The Organization of The United Methodist Church

Revised 1989 Edition

Jack M. Tuell

ABINGDON PRESS   Nashville

The
Organization
of
The United
Methodist
Church

THE ORGANIZATION OF
THE UNITED METHODIST CHURCH
REVISED EDITION

Copyright © *1970, 1973, 1977, 1982, 1985, 1989 by Abingdon Press*

This book is printed on acid-free paper.

Library of Congress Cataloging in Publication Data

TUELL, JACK M., 1923-
   The organization of The United Methodist Church.
   Includes index.
   1. United Methodist Church (U.S.)—Government.
   2. Methodist Church—Government. I. Title.
BX8382.2.Z5T83 1985   262'.076   84-28287

ISBN 0-687-29446-0

Scripture quotations unless otherwise noted are from the Revised Standard Version
of the Bible, copyrighted 1946, 1952, 1971, © 1973, by the Division of Christian
Education of the National Council of the Churches of Christ in the U.S.A., and
used by permission.

MANUFACTURED BY THE PARTHENON PRESS AT
NASHVILLE, TENNESSEE, UNITED STATES OF AMERICA

To my colleagues of the
Pacific Northwest Annual Conference
and of the Portland and Los Angeles Areas

PREFACE

The 1988 General Conference of The United Methodist Church, which met in Saint Louis in late April and early May, was characterized by the media as "calm." What contributed to the sense of peacefulness and goodwill that marked these sessions?

Strangely enough, the advance of technology had a part. For the first time, delegates voted electronically—*and* anonymously. The social pressure and stress associated with identifying how one stood on controversial issues was removed. Each ten-second voting period produced a strange quiet as delegates gazed at the television screen, waiting for it to tell them what they had done. The overall impact during the ten days was a lowering of anxiety levels.

There was an acceptance of the idea that The United Methodist Church is committed to historic Christianity. This was seen in the report of the new hymnal, which, while proposing many changes toward greater inclusiveness, maintained a strong basic commitment to evangelical Christianity. This acceptance also was evident in the action concerning homosexuality: the Conference rather strongly affirmed its position of affirming the rights and dignity of homosexual persons, while at the same time not being willing to affirm homosexual behavior as normative. But the Conference approved a major study on this theme, indicating a felt need to know more on this complex subject.

The Holy Spirit was present. Nowhere was this more evident

than in what happened to the doctrinal statement. Before the General Conference, many had predicted there would be a major division, even schism, over the proposed new statement. But in true conciliar fashion, persons of opposing views came together and worked through their differences to produce a document that secured overwhelming support. Thus a potential schism was transformed into a heartwarming affirmation of faith and unity. Surely God's spirit was at work.

At any rate, a "calm" General Conference does not produce drastic changes in *The Book of Discipline*. And since this book is basically a commentary on that book, there are relatively few changes in this edition. But this book is offered in the hope that it may illuminate and clarify what is admittedly a complex structure. May it be accepted in that spirit.

JACK M. TUELL
Whidbey Island
Summer 1988

CONTENTS

Chapter I

FOUNDATIONS

In order to understand how a church or any institution is organized, it is essential to understand the foundations upon which the institution is built. For instance, a Roman Catholic or an Episcopalian may find the United Methodist practice of removing members from the rolls after three years of inactivity hard to understand, and perhaps downright offensive. They may feel that this is not the way a church ought to treat its constituents who have been baptized into the family of God, and who deserve better than to be "put out of the family" in such a seemingly unceremonious way. But a look at history soon helps them understand why our church functions this way; for United Methodism began not as a church, but as a disciplined religious society. So when people became Methodists in the days of John Wesley, they were not joining a church—they were probably already members of the Church of England—rather, they were joining a society (what we might call today a "small group") for the express purpose of bettering their spiritual condition. So the rules were strict and the discipline tight, and it is out of such "societies" that The United Methodist Church of today has evolved. This historical background has, for better or for worse, left its imprint upon United Methodism, and one of the places we see it is in our attitude toward the termination of church membership because of inactivity.

The Book of Discipline of The United Methodist Church (1988)

11

is organized in such a way that these "foundations" of our organization are set forth at the outset in a "Historical Statement" and in Paragraphs 1-76. This portion of the *Discipline* forms the basis for this chapter.

Historical Origins

The Uniting Conference of The United Methodist Church, held at Dallas, Texas, in April of 1968, brought together into one church two great Protestant churches—The Methodist Church and The Evangelical United Brethren Church. These two churches, similar in doctrinal outlook as well as in matters of organization, may well have come together years ago if it had not been for a language difference—the Evangelical United Brethren did their work among the German-speaking people, while the Methodists worked among the English-speaking population. With these language barriers now gone, all real reasons for continuing separation ceased to exist, and the union took place. A brief look at these two streams of church life is in order.

The Evangelical United Brethren Church was itself the result of a union consummated in 1946 of the Church of the United Brethren in Christ and the Evangelical Church. The spiritual father of the United Brethren was Philip William Otterbein, an ordained minister of the German Reformed Church, who, along with Martin Boehm, began preaching to the German-speaking settlers of the middle colonies of young America in the late 1700s and early 1800s. There is a remarkable similarity between the work of Otterbein and the work of John Wesley. Both saw a society desperately in need of the gospel; both emphasized the necessity of a vital and experiential relationship to God; both began their work with the intent not to establish new churches, but to bring about a renewal of faith within established churches; both eventually saw the need of establishing a church in America; both were gifted, natural leaders of great energy and conviction.

The societies grew rapidly under Otterbein's leadership, and meetings of the ministers were held in 1789 in Baltimore, Maryland, and in 1791 in Paradise Township, York County,

12

Pennsylvania. Starting with the meeting on September 25, 1800, in Frederick County, Maryland, these meetings were held annually. It was not until 1815, however, when the first General Conference was held near Mt. Pleasant, Pennsylvania, that a book of discipline appeared. In 1841, a constitution was adopted, and though it was amended in 1889, the Church of the United Brethren in Christ functioned and grew under this constitution until its merger with the Evangelical Church in 1946.

The Evangelical Church had its beginnings with the work of Jacob Albright at about the same time the United Brethren were organizing. Albright was not an ordained minister, but a tilemaker and a farmer. However, his view of religion as being primarily a vital, personal, experiential relationship to God put him in complete agreement with Otterbein and Wesley. After his own conversion in 1791, he began preaching and gathering some followers, who met in their first council in 1803. In 1807 the preachers held the first of what were to become annual meetings, and in 1809 a book of discipline was adopted. At the first General Conference, the name "the Evangelical Association" was adopted. This was in 1816, and the association grew and thrived through the century. In 1891 a split occurred within the church, with one group of ministers and laity leaving to form the United Evangelical Church. This new church held its first General Conference in 1894, but almost from its inception there were those who felt that the two branches should be reunited, and in 1922, only thirty-one years after the original split, the two churches came back together to form a united body, the Evangelical Church.

These two churches, the Church of the United Brethren in Christ and the Evangelical Church, had worked side by side in America, both originally among German-speaking people and both very much alike in outlook and structure. So it was a natural thing that in 1933 representatives of the two groups should begin negotiations which culminated in 1946 with the formation of one church, The Evangelical United Brethren Church. It was this church which was to join a plan of union which resulted in the formation of The United Methodist Church in Dallas in 1968. The other party to that plan of union was The Methodist

13

Church, which had its beginnings in England with the work of John Wesley in the 1700s. Born into a parsonage home in 1703, Wesley grew up to become the outstanding religious figure of his century. He secured his education at Oxford University, and was ordained a clergyman of the Church of England. While at Oxford he and some companions formed a small group for prayer, study, and service to people in need, and, because they set out such a rigorous and methodical schedule for their activities, they were derisively referred to by some of their more worldly fellow students as "Methodists." But Wesley soon found, like Paul and Martin Luther before him, that striving for salvation by the keeping of rules and regulations, by trying harder even to the extent of going off to America as a missionary to the Indians, was of no avail. Finally, on the evening of May 24, 1738, at a prayer meeting held in Aldersgate Street in London, Wesley had a personal experience in which, he said, "I felt my heart strangely warmed, and I felt that I did trust in Christ, in him alone for salvation, and that he had saved *me* from the law of sin and death." So, religion had become for John Wesley what it was later to become for Philip William Otterbein and Jacob Albright: a direct, personal, unforgettable experience of the presence and love of God, an experience so overwhelming that it had to be communicated to others.

John Wesley went out from the Aldersgate experience to begin the preaching, organizing, and administrative work which was to result, at the time of his death over fifty years later, in some half a million souls in England called Methodists, and an infant church in America. Wesley remained a clergyman of the Church of England until his death, and insisted that his societies in England should remain that—societies—and not become a church. However, after the American Revolution had taken place, he recognized that the Church of England could no longer function in America and that an ordained clergy was needed. His efforts to get the Bishop of London to ordain some of his preachers failed, so finally Wesley himself ordained two men and set aside Dr. Thomas Coke as a superintendent for the work in America, giving him directions to ordain Francis Asbury a second superintendent.

On December 24, 1784, Dr. Coke met with about sixty

preachers in Baltimore, Maryland, and organized the Methodist Episcopal Church. At this "Christmas Conference" all essential steps to organizing a church were carried out, and Francis Asbury emerged as dominant leader and "bishop," a term whose use Wesley was opposed to, but which quickly became common usage among American Methodists.

Two important divisions were to occur in this rapidly growing frontier-following young church. A group of persons concerned with lay representation in the church left it in 1828 to form the Methodist Protestant Church. In 1844 another division occurred, this time between north and south. The issue was interpreted by some to be over slavery, and by some to be over the powers of the General Conference and the episcopacy. Almost from the time of these divisions there were forces at work to bring about a reunion and, after years of negotiation, this took place on May 10, 1939, when the Methodist Episcopal Church, the Methodist Episcopal Church, South, and the Methodist Protesant Church came back together to form The Methodist Church. It was this church which, in April of 1968, at Dallas, Texas, united with The Evangelical United Brethren to form The United Methodist Church.

Theological Affirmations

What kind of theological claims or affirmations do United Methodists make about their church? What do they believe it to be? How do they believe it fits in with the plans and the will of God? What are its relationships to other churches? Answers to these questions provide important foundation stones for an understanding of the organization of the church.

The Preamble to the Constitution sets forth some of the answers to these questions:

The Church is a community of all true believers under the Lordship of Christ. It is the redeemed and redeeming fellowship in which the Word of God is preached by persons divinely called, and the Sacraments are duly administered according to Christ's own appointment. Under the

15

discipline of the Holy Spirit the Church seeks to provide for the maintenance of worship, the edification of believers, and the redemption of the world.

The Church of Jesus Christ exists in and for the world, and its very dividedness is a hindrance to its mission in that world. (page 19, *Discipline*)

This statement is a skillful blending of at least four other official statements about the church. One of these is the definition of the church contained in Article XIII of the Articles of Religion of The Methodist Church (page 64). The second is the definition of the church set forth in Article V of the Confession of Faith of The Evangelical United Brethren Church (page 70). The third is in Paragraphs 201, 202, and 203 of the *Discipline* concerning the local church. Paragraph 203 makes explicit what is only implicit in the earlier statements, that the persons "have been baptized." It also makes clear that a local congregation "is also an inherent part of the Church Universal, which is composed of all who accept Jesus Christ as Lord and Savior, and which in the Apostles' Creed we declare to be the holy catholic Church." The fourth official statement appears in the Order for Confirmation and Reception into the Church (*The Book of Worship*, page 12). This statement also conforms to the statement in the Preamble to the Constitution, adding the idea that the church "will be preserved to the end of time."

A number of important theological affirmations are contained in this Preamble to the Constitution. *"The Church is a community.* . . . " This makes it clear that the church is not a building, it is not a certain organizational structure, it is not a denomination; the church is people, consciously and purposefully joined together. *". . . of all true believers."* This indicates that what binds the people into a community are certain shared convictions, which are not spelled out here but are presumed to be the historic beliefs of the Christian church. *". . . under the Lordship of Christ."* There is really only one head of the church, and that is Jesus Christ himself. Churches may elect officers and authorities to exercise certain important functions on behalf of the community, but

16

always it is recognized that the only true head is Jesus Christ himself.

"*It is the redeemed and redeeming fellowship.* . . . " Here is revealed something basic about both the nature and the purpose of the community. It is redeemed; that is, it is composed of persons who have recognized their incompleteness apart from God, have confessed their faith in Christ as Savior and Lord, and have become a part of the community of his followers. They are redeemed in that their lives have been set on the way which God intends for them. But the fellowship is redeeming in at least two senses: first, the redeemed (the members of the church) are in continuous need of redeeming—thus redemption is always more of a continuing process than it is a completed transaction; in United Methodist parlance, we are always "going on" to perfection. The second meaning of redeeming is an evangelistic one; while the redeeming process is going on with the redeemed, it is also reaching out to the world, through both the words and the acts of the fellowship. Such words and acts constitute the ministry of the redeemed fellowship.

"*. . . in which the Word of God is preached by persons divinely called.*" One of the central emphases of this community, one of its marks, is preaching—preaching the Word of God. United Methodism's founder, John Wesley, was one of the great preachers of his time, and the heritage of strong and vital preaching has been with us from the very beginning. Furthermore, it is a long held conviction of United Methodists that preachers are called by God. The first question of a person taking the first step toward the United Methodist ministry used to be, "Do you believe yourself to be divinely called to preach the gospel?" But it is important to note here that our church has never attempted to put a particular interpretation on just what a "call" is, believing that God is capable of calling persons in an infinite variety of ways.

"*. . . and the Sacraments are duly administered according to Christ's own appointment.*" United Methodism shares with Protestantism in general the recognition of two sacraments, as compared to seven recognized by Roman Catholicism. The criterion for a sacrament, according to most Protestant theolo-

17

gians, is that it be something which Christ specifically told his followers to do. So, we recognize baptism (Matt. 28:19) and the Lord's Supper, or Holy Communion (Matt. 26:26-28). United Methodism also shares with the Protestant community the conviction that while the sacraments are very important means of grace, they are not the sole means of grace. While Roman Catholic views about baptism are undergoing change in recognizing differing ways in which baptism may come to persons, the traditional view has held baptism absolutely essential for salvation. United Methodism rejects that position, on the grounds that this is an unwarranted limitation upon the limitless power of God and contrary to the very nature of God as revealed in Christ, which is love. Does this mean that we believe the sacraments to be unimportant? By no means! Baptism remains the indispensable first step of a person into the Christian community, and the Holy Communion provides us with the bread and wine which feed us as we travel along the Way, a constant reminder of him who is not only the Way, but the Truth and the Life.

"Under the discipline of the Holy Spirit. . . ." It is appropriate that the word "discipline" should appear in this definition, for it is an old and honored word in United Methodism. It is often used as a title to describe the book of rules we live by within the church, but that is only one expression of the broader discipline referred to here. This is the discipline of a people under orders—a people acting out together their response to the commission laid on them by our Lord himself: "Go into all the world and preach the gospel to the whole creation" (Mark 16:15). The usual objection to discipline is that it is binding and restrictive, but the marvelous thing about the "discipline of the Holy Spirit" is that it frees! It is this discipline we are talking about when we sing, "Make me a captive, Lord, And then I shall be free." While it could not be claimed that the discipline practiced by United Methodism has always come under the discipline of the Holy Spirit, it is true that the spiritual children of the methodical John Wesley have enjoyed a freedom not always enjoyed by their Christian colleagues of other denominations. This is especially true of the ministry, where the free pulpit and the relatively free-swinging ways of United

18

Methodist ministers are often the envy of their ministerial colleagues. It's the kind of freedom worth giving up a pipe for. *". . . the Church seeks to provide for the maintenance of worship, the edification of believers, and the redemption of the world."* The language here is similar to that in the confirmation ritual, and serves as a condensed "job description" of the church. There is some significance to the "maintenance of worship" coming first, since worship is the starting point for everything else the church does. It is no small thing to consider how the church has, through the centuries, provided regular worship services for its people, week in and week out, year in and year out, in the open country, in hamlets, in villages, towns, cities, and great urban centers. I marvel when I think that the church I once served as pastor has provided the opportunity for worship to the community every Sunday for over one hundred years! It is so easy to take worship for granted, yet its centrality to the whole mission of the church is amply demonstrated both theologically and historically. So, the worship of God as he has been revealed to us through Christ is the indispensable first task of the church.

"The edification of believers" points to the educational task of the church. It is not mutually exclusive from worship, but overlaps it, and takes place, in part, in the "worship service." The recent emphasis being placed on adult education in the church is a rediscovery of the truth that the edification of believers is not something which stops when a person graduates from a high school Sunday school class or finishes a confirmation class, but is one of the central, continuing, basic tasks of the church. The increasingly obvious fact that so many persons on the rolls of our churches are appallingly ignorant of some of the most elemental truths of the Christian faith points to the church's neglect of this important task of "edifying believers."

"And the redemption of the world." The Preamble spoke earlier of the church as the "redeemed and redeeming fellowship." Now it makes clear the scope of that redeeming work: nothing less than the whole world! What a job description! The word "redemption" is used here rather than the word "conversion" as in the ritual for confirmation of The Methodist Church. "Redemption" is perhaps

19

the better word here, for it carries some broader implications than "conversion." Conversion is often thought of as carrying strictly individual connotations of a particular kind of religious experience; hence, the conversion of the world may be envisioned as the one-by-one salvation of every soul on the face of the earth. Now, the word "redemption" includes this concept, but it is broader, carrying with it a social concern that persons might be redeemed from the squalor of poverty, racism, prejudice, and injustice. Thus, it is a word which carries overtones both individual and social, and indicates that the church can never rest as long as there are persons in need of the gospel. This individual and social approach is faithful to John Wesley himself and to United Methodism at its best through the years.

"The Church of Jesus Christ exists in and for the world. . . ." This is really a caution against institutional self-centeredness and ambition. Always there is the temptation to think of the church as an end in itself. This temptation seems to grow more pressing as a church grows in size; with greater institutional needs and the need for a division of labor, more and more personnel are devoting their time and energy to the institutional needs of the church rather than to a direct carrying out of the mission of the church to the world. Thus the church develops a bureaucracy with all of the particular problems which go with it. This is not to suggest that we don't need a bureaucracy; the fact is that we do if the church is to do its task in our world today. It is only to suggest that all of us in the church, at every level (the problems of bureaucracy can be just as pervasive in the local church as in the higher echelons), need constantly to read and reread this phrase from the Preamble to our Constitution: "The Church of Jesus Christ exists in and for the world."

". . . *and its very dividedness is a hindrance to its mission in that world.*" This is a healthy admission of the incompleteness of the church in its present organizational structures. It is another way of saying that we have a long way to go before we begin to fulfill the prayer of our Lord "that they may all be one . . . that the world may believe." This statement puts its finger on the overriding reason and motivation for us to overcome our dividedness—such dividedness gets in the way of our doing our job. The world says,

20

"You're preaching a gospel of love and reconciliation? Why don't you get together yourselves?" And as long as we maintain our dividedness, the world is never going to believe us. Unity in spirit is not enough; we within the church may understand this kind of invisible unity (although it may also serve as a convenient cloak for our continuing idolatry of some of our cherished sectarian ideas), but the world, for whom the church exists, does not understand it. So it is important and highly significant that these theological affirmations about the church, contained in the Preamble to our Constitution, should end on this provisional and incomplete note. In our structures as in our personal lives, we are "going on to perfection."

The Constitution

After the Preamble, with its theological affirmations about the nature of the church, the body of the Constitution follows with five basic divisions. There is a certain logic to these divisions, with Division One setting forth a series of general statements about the church, its name, its nature, the legal status of its properties; Divisions Two, Three, and Four then roughly correspond to the three branches of government in the United States, the legislative, the executive, and the judicial; and Division Five is concerned with the procedures for amending the Constitution.

Division One begins with a declaration of union, indicating formally, for all the world to see and know, that what were two churches—The Evangelical United Brethren Church and The Methodist Church—are now and shall be one church. The intent of this first article is to establish historical continuity. Its intent is to describe what has happened in the union of the two churches, not as two former churches dying and a new church springing up, but as two churches, formerly separated, now continuing their streams of life within a new and larger stream. Thus, the church is "something new," but it is also "something old." As a new church, it is freed to do many things which may not have been possible under the two former churches; in many ways it is a new creation. But Article I is a constant reminder that this new church is also the inheritor of great traditions of long standing. Thus, the leadership

21

of the new church is in the unique position of being able to choose the best of two worlds, the old and the new.

Article II gives a name to the church, The United Methodist Church. This was a matter of some contention at the General Conferences of the two churches in 1966 in Chicago, with many Methodist delegates being very reluctant to give up their simple and direct name, "The Methodist Church." However, the E. U. B. delegates felt strongly that the name of the church needed to be a new one, in order accurately to reflect that what was to happen was a union of two churches, and not simply the absorption of a smaller church into a larger one. The Methodist delegates were persuaded of the importance of this point, and the new name was agreed upon. The name has enjoyed warm and widespread acceptance throughout the new church.

The adotpion of Article III, which establishes the Articles of Religion of The Methodist Church and the Confession of Faith of the E. U. B. Church as definitive for The United Methodist Church, was made possible only by what lawyers refer to as a "legal fiction." By this we mean that in the Constitution of The Methodist Church there was a provision listed in the Restrictive Rules which said: "The General Conference shall not revoke, alter, or change our Articles of Religion or establish any new standards or rules of doctrine contrary to our present existing and established standards of doctrine." This provision is carried over intact into the new Constitution.

The big question was, Does the addition of the entire Confession of Faith of the E. U. B. Church constitute an "altering" of the Methodist Articles of Religion or the establishing of "new standards or rules of doctrine contrary to our present existing and established standards of doctrine"? Any examination of the two documents reveals that it undoubtedly does. For instance, Article XII of the E. U. B. Confession of Faith contains these words: "We believe in the resurrection of the dead; the righteous to life eternal and the wicked to endless condemnation." There is nothing in the Articles of Religion which spells this out, particularly the last phrase concerning "endless condemnation." This, then, is the introduction of a new element into the Articles of Religion, which surely

22

constitutes an altering of them. Another example is Article XIV of the Confession of Faith, concerning the Lord's Day. This is all new and additional material which is not covered in the Articles of Religion, and must be considered as altering them. However, the Articles of Religion were not formally amended (the language still remains the same in the text), and the argument could be made that the addition of the Confession of Faith of the E.U.B. Church did not establish any "new standards or rules of doctrine *contrary* to our present existing and established standards of doctrine." At any rate, the two General Conferences in 1966 adopted the two doctrinal statements side by side, and adopted a resolution in which they "deemed them to be congruent." This was the key phrase and the one which would be construed by some to be a legal fiction—that is, a way to accomplish a desired legal end which does not correspond exactly with the reality of the situation.

At the time of this action by the General Conferences, the matter was then referred to the Judicial Council for a ruling, and they, quite rightly, declined to become involved in deciding the theological questions of whether or not the Articles of Religion and the Confession of Faith were in conflict. They felt this was a matter for the General Conference to decide, and if it "deemed them to be congruent," that was the end of the matter. So the legal barriers were overcome, and the official statements of doctrine of both the uniting churches have become the standards for the new church.

This solution was an expedient one in bringing about the union of the two churches, but it really did not satisfy everyone. As a result, the Uniting Conference in Dallas established a Theological Study Commission on Doctrine and Doctrinal Standards. The report of this commission, overwhelmingly adopted by the 1972 General Conference, left the Articles of Religion and the Confession of Faith intact, but supplemented them and gave direction to continued theological exploration within the church through the reaffirmation of Wesley's guidelines of "Scripture, tradition, experience, and reason."

The 1972 statement served the church well, but there began to be a growing dissatisfaction with it, mostly on two grounds: First, it was felt it did not adequately lift up the primacy of scripture;

second, that in its emphasis on "pluralism," it was giving an impression of a theological indifferentism. As a result of these concerns, the 1984 General Conference authorized a quadrennial study on "Our Theological Task." This study commission brought to the 1988 General Conference a new document, which, after some amendment in legislative committee, was overwhelmingly accepted. This new statement now appears as Paragraphs 66–69 in the *1988 Book of Discipline*.

Paragraph 4 starts with a theological affirmation which makes it clear that we believe The United Methodist Church to be a part of "the Church Universal which is one Body in Christ." Because this is true, the church must be inclusive—open to all persons without regard to "race, color, national origin, or economic condition . . . in any local church in the connection." This makes it absolutely clear that the doors of every United Methodist local church everywhere are to be open to all people, and that anyone who bars another on grounds of race is in violation of the Constitution of The United Methodist Church. Certainly the spirit of this provision is violated as much by the person who gives a cold shoulder to a worshiper of another race as it is by the usher who stands in the door and tells a worshiper that he or she would probably like it better at the church down the street. In spite of this clearly stated position of the church, it is true that a great deal of segregation of a *de facto* nature exists at the level of the local church.

There is an easy and glib answer to this which says, "This is the way people want it—this is what they choose to do—this is where they feel at home." But it is a terrible admission of failure within the church that our attitudes have been such that large numbers of people do not feel at home in our midst. During the 1972-76 quadrennium, the last remaining district and Annual Conference segregated structures were eliminated. This was the culmination of a long, and on the whole a truly remarkable, process of accomplishment which played an important part in the larger struggle for racial justice taking place in the United States.

Paragraph 5 is concerned with ecumenical relations and reiterates what has been made clear earlier—our view of United

Methodism as being incomplete, provisional, unfinished, "going on to perfection." This constitutional provision makes it clear that our church is committed to a full acceptance of the gift of unity, as it may be expressed both through councils of churches and through future organic unions with other denominations.

Division Two of the Constitution is entitled *Organization*. This seems like an overly broad title, since the entire Constitution deals with organization. What Division Two deals with is the conference system of The United Methodist Church, which roughly corresponds to the legislative branch of civil government. Since a later chapter will be devoted to a discussion of the conferences, we with limit this section to only the constitutional aspects of the conference system.

THE GENERAL CONFERENCE. The General Conference is the supreme legislative body of United Methodism. It is made up of not less than six hundred nor more than one thousand delegates, on a formula spelled out in a later section of the *Discipline*. Half of the delegates are ministers and half are laypersons, elected by their Annual Conferences. The General Conference meets once every four years in the month of April or May. The Constitution also provides for a special session to be called by the Council of Bishops or in such other way as the General Conference may determine (Par. 13).

How is the number of delegates from an Annual Conference decided? Should it be "one person, one vote"? And if so, should the ratio of representation be based on the number of ministers in an Annual Conference or on the number of church members? The Methodist Church traditionally had based representation on the number of ministers, while the E.U.B. Church had based it on church membership as well. The result in the Constitution of the new church is the E.U.B. "two-factor basis" as set forth in Paragraph 14, in which representation is based on both the number of ministers and the number of church members, each factor being equal. The Constitution also provides that every Annual Conference or Provisional Annual Conference shall be entitled to at least one ministerial and one lay delegate even though it should

25

be too small to have representation under the formula. So, the principle of "one person, one vote" is adhered to quite closely in the election of ministerial delegates. "One person, one vote" also applies fairly closely to the election of lay delegates, at least as related to each lay delegate being the representative of approximately the same number of lay members of the Annual Conference who elected the delegate. However, the two-factor basis could work to distort the "one person, one vote" principle somewhat. For instance, an Annual Conference which had a high proportion of its pastoral charges served by full ministerial members, plus a large number of full ministerial members in special appointments (thus maximizing the factor of ministerial membership) and a high average membership per pastoral charge (thus maximizing the factor of church membership) might find that it could elect one lay delegate to General Conference for every fifty lay members of the Annual Conference; while an Annual Conference with the opposite set of circumstances might find that it could elect one lay delegate to General Conference for every ninety lay members.

When we go one step further and ask how "one person, one vote" applies to the number of church members each lay delegate to General Conference represents, we hazard the guess that there may be an even wider variation. This is because the lay member at Annual Conference casting a vote for a lay delegate to General Conference may be representing one hundred church members in the local church, or he or she may be representing one thousand. So, adherence to the "one person, one vote" idea is only roughly approximated in the election of delegates to the General Conference. However, weighing out all the various and sometimes conflicting demands which the democratic ideal places upon a church structure, it is doubtful if a much fairer or more democratic or representative system of electing delegates to the General Conference could be devised.

What are the constitutional powers of the General Conference? Paragraph 15 makes this sweeping statement: "The General Conference shall have full legislative power over all matters distinctively connectional, and in the exercise of this power shall have authority as follows": And here follows a list of fifteen areas in which the General Conference is given power to act. The grant of power is broad and sweeping, including that of defining the terms of church membership and the ministry, determining all the various structures of the church, and guaranteeing the rightful place of all members in these structures, regardless of race or status. The last of the enumerated powers is so broad as to remove any doubt as to the tremendous powers of the General Conference: "To enact such other legislation as may be necessary, subject to the limitations and restrictions of the Constitution of the Church." There were arguments in an earlier day over the powers of the General Conference as over against the "reserved powers" of the Annual Conferences, similar in nature to the arguments which raged at one time over states' rights against federal power. Both arguments have been resolved in the same manner, with federal power prevailing on the civil scene and the powers of the General Conference prevailing on the church scene.

This does not mean, of course, that the General Conference is free to do anything it wants; it is "subject to the limitations and restrictions of the Constitution." Some of these restrictions are because of specific grants of power made in the Constitution to other groups. For instance, the General Conference could not act as a judicial body, because these functions have been delegated to the Judicial Council under the Constitution; nor could it decide to ordain some ministers, because the function of ordaining ministers is placed in the hands of the Annual Conferences by the Constitution; nor could it elect bishops, because the Constitution has given this job expressly to Jurisdictional and Central Conferences. But aside from these and similar other constitutional grants of power to other groups within the church, the General Conference, subject to the Restrictive Rules which will be discussed below, has an extremely wide scope of power and as such occupies a place as one of the most powerful and important ecclesiastical bodies on the face of the earth.

The Restrictive Rules (Pars. 16-20) are intended as restrictions on the power of the General Conference in certain areas. The motivation for some of these restrictions (Articles I, III, V, and VI)

27

was the conviction of early Methodist leaders that some things were so important and some principles so basic that they should be put beyond even the power of the General Conference to change. One of the restrictions (II) came with the Methodist-E.U.B. union. This puts the former E.U.B. statements of basic doctrine on a par with the former Methodist statements. One restrictive rule, Article IV, seems to be in the nature of a bill of rights which ensures certain rights of due process to ministers and members of our church.

Looking at the Restrictive Rules *ad seriatim*, we see that Articles I and II are meant to keep the General Conference from tinkering with the basic doctrines as set forth in the Articles of Religion of the former Methodist Church and the Confession of Faith of the former E.U.B. Church. Many persons today would debate the wisdom of making our official formulations of faith so difficult to change. They would say, "We have no hesitation in recommending new translations of the Bible itself rather than insisting on the King James Version; why should we cling to official theological formulations which are couched in King James English?" As a practical matter, what happens is that more and more pastors and teachers virtually ignore these basic statements as they endeavor to present Christian truth, treating them largely as matters of historical interest. This is regrettable.

A Theological Study Commission on Doctrine and Doctrinal Standards was created in 1968 which was given authority to "undertake the preparation of a contemporary formulation of doctrine and belief, *in supplementation to all antecedent formulations.*" The report of the Study Commission adopted by the General Conference of 1972, as well as the 1988 document on our theological task which replaced it, includes the Articles of Religion and the Confession of Faith mentioned in the first and second Restrictive Rules. Does this mean that these two statements, considered archaic by many, are frozen permanently and irrevocably into our Constitution? Not necessarily. These two restrictive rules *can* be changed, but it would take a three-fourths vote of all the members of the Annual Conference to accomplish this, in addition to a two-thirds vote of the General Conference

(Par. 62). In other words, it would take an overwhelming desire for change in order to change these two rules, but perhaps this near unanimity is essential when matters as fundamental as doctrine are to be changed. Evidently the framers of our Constitution believed this.

The third Restrictive Rule prohibits actions by the General Conference which would "do away with episcopacy or destroy the plan of our itinerant general superintendency." This is a recognition of the co-equal standing of the episcopacy as one of three branches, along with the conferences and the judiciary in our church. This does not mean that the General Conference cannot pass rules and regulations governing the episcopacy; in fact, it is expressly given this power in the Constitution (Par. 15.5). What it does mean is that the General Conference is without power to enact legislation whose effect is to destroy the institution of the episcopacy or to change its essential nature. This line between permissible legislation of the General Conference on the subject of the episcopacy and that which is not permissible is not an easy one to draw, because it is based upon not only a series of judicial precedents established by General Conferences and judicial bodies of the constituent churches over a period of years, but also on a body of tradition which has built up over nearly two centuries. There will, without doubt, be future Judicial Council decisions in this area as the General Conference tests and probes its powers of regulation of the episcopacy under Paragraph 15.5 of the Constitution, and walks the borderline of this third Restrictive Rule. The rule itself, of course, could be changed by a two-thirds vote of the General Conference and a two-thirds vote of all the members of the Annual Conferences.

The fourth Restrictive Rule is a guarantee to both ministers and laity that their privileges shall not be taken from them without the basic right of a trial before their peers and a chance for an appeal. Elsewhere in the *Discipline* there is legislation implementing this constitutional provision (Pars. 2620-2626).

The fifth Restrictive Rule forbids the General Conference to "revoke or change the General Rules of Our United Societies." These General Rules, to be discussed later in this chapter, are the

29

rules promulgated by John Wesley for the religious societies he created in England in the eighteenth century. They are a series of strict personal rules, appropriate for highly disciplined small groups such as the societies of Wesley's day. They are extremely interesting from a historical point of view, giving insight into some of the dynamics of the early Methodist movement. However, from a legal and juridical point of view it is highly unlikely that they are regarded as being rules presently in force in The United Methodist Church. If this view is accepted, then the Restrictive Rule poses no problems, since no one would be about to change the rules of an organization which lives only in history.

The sixth Restrictive Rule draws a line around the proceeds of the publishing business of the church, and makes it clear that the General Conference cannot appropriate any of these funds for any purpose other than ministerial pensioners, their spouses, widows or widowers, or children. It has been a rule in effect from the earliest days of our publishing work, and has been a great source of strength in the funding of pensions.

In summary, the General Conference, as set forth in the Constitution, remains the most poweful and important body in United Methodism, despite the six Restrictive Rules, and despite other constitutional delegations of power which somewhat limit is authority.

JURISDICTIONAL CONFERENCES. The Jurisdictional Conferences (Pars. 21-25) are regional bodies, five in number in the United States, with specified powers and duties spelled out in Paragraph 25 of the Constitution. The concept of Jurisdictional Conferences came into being in 1939 at the time of the reunion of the three branches of Methodism into The Methodist Church. At that time, in addition to the five regional jurisdictions, there was also the Central Jurisdiction, which was a grouping of all the Negro Annual Conferences that had been created by the Methodist Episcopal Church in the period following the Civil War. The Central Jurisdiction was the center of controversy from its beginning, and by the time of the birth of The United Methodist Church was eliminated from the structure, with the local churches and Annual

Conferences becoming a part of the regional jurisdiction in which they were situated.

Undoubtedly the most important function carried out by the Jurisdictional Conferences is the election of bishops, although the Jurisdictional Conference is also given under the Constitution the right to carry on the program of the church within the Jurisdiction, to determine boundaries of the Annual Conferences, and to appoint a Committee on Appeals. Some jurisdictions, notably the Southeastern, have developed their jurisdictional structure into a considerable instrument in the program of the church, while others have developed only a minimal organization, content to let the Jurisdictional Conference serve almost exclusively as a device for electing bishops.

Some debate continues within the church concerning the value of the jurisdictional system, and some of these arguments will be set forth in a later chapter.

CENTRAL CONFERENCES. Paragraphs 26-29 of the Constitution deal with Central Conferences and the role and responsibilities of bishops in them. Central Conferences perform about the same functions as Jurisdictional Conferences, except that they are located in other countries than the United States. However, because of their location and their need to adapt to the needs there, they are accorded a larger measure of freedom to work out their own structures than is the case of the Jurisdictional Conferences. One of the most dramatic evidences of this is seen in the fact that, while life tenure of bishops is the prevailing rule in United Methodism and is mandatory in the Jurisdictional Conferences, the Central Conferences are given freedom to establish whatever tenure they wish for their bishops (par. 53). Even with this large measure of freedom, however, there has been some movement in recent years for the church overseas to move away from the Central Conference structure and to ask for full autonomy, although this has been by no means universal. In fact, several churches outside the United States have recently come into the United Methodist structure.

ANNUAL CONFERENCES. "The Annual Conference is the basic body in the Church." This quotation from Paragraph 36 indicates

31

the central place which the Annual Conference holds in the total structure of The United Methodist Church. Part of the reason for this is historical—John Wesley was holding Annual Conferences of his preachers long before there was any such thing as a local Methodist church. When Otterbein and Asbury met in Annual Conferences with the early preachers in America, there was more substance to the Annual Conference than there was to the idea of a local church. That is, the preachers were itinerants, moving from place to place, preaching to groups of people who came to hear them. These groups later became societies and then local churches, but at the beginning they were just groups of people who came to hear an itinerant preacher. So the Annual Conference has a certain primacy in United Methodist history; it was not a gathering together of local churches, but a body of preachers under orders. It is partly for these historical reasons that the Annual Conference occupies such an important and unique place in our structure. It is also because in a church structure which we label "connectional," it is the Annual Conference which is the primary "connector" of the local churches, and to which every local church and pastor is related. The basic nature of the Annual Conference is also made clear in the Constitution (Par. 36), where the right of voting on constitutional amendments, the election of General Conference delegates, the decision on all matters related to admission to the ministry, conference relations of ministers, and ordination are all reserved to the Annual Conference.

The Annual Conference is made up of two classes of members: ministerial and lay. The basis for membership differs in the two classes. Lay membership is based on the principle of representation of each local church or, more correctly, each pastoral charge, which may consist of more than one local church but be served by one pastor. Each pastoral charge is entitled to elect one lay member, unless the charge is served full time by more than one minister under appointment; in that case the charge may elect as many lay members as it has ministers appointed to it. The principle of ministerial membership is entirely different, and not related to representation of the local church. Ministerial membership is conferred by the ministerial members in full connection with the

Annual Conference, and is for life. Thus, while ministers who are pastors of charges are equally balanced by lay members, ministers who are district superintendents, or who are retired, or who are on special appointment are also voting members of the conference and are not matched by a corresponding lay member. Therefore, an Annual Conference may have more ministerial than lay members representing local churches.

However, it is possible for the opposite to be true in a conference where, because of a shortage of ministers, many pulpits are filled by part-time local pastors. In such a case, the pastoral charge is still entitled to elect its lay member to the conference, but its part-time local pastor is not entitled to vote as a ministerial member. However, the Judicial Council may approve the legislation passed by the 1988 General Conference to allow an Annual Conference, under certain conditions and by a 2/3 vote, to grant part-time local pastors the vote.

These factors tend to balance each other out somewhat, and the approximate equal representation of lay and ministerial members of the Annual Conference is reasonably maintained throughout United Methodism. The balance has also been helped by the inclusion in the Constitution of the conference president of United Methodist Women, the conference president of United Methodist Men, the president of the conference youth organization, the conference lay leader and two young persons under twenty-five from each district, as voting members of the Annual Conference. A constitutional amendment adopted in the 1972-76 quadrennium allows for Annual Conferences to provide for additional lay members in order to equalize lay and clergy representation. A constitutional amendment voted by the 1984 General Conference and by the Annual Conferences gave diaconal ministers membership in the Annual Conference as laity.

The qualifications for delegates to the General, Jurisdictional, and Central Conferences are spelled out in Paragraphs 38 and 39. Eligible ministers must have been members in a conference for at least four years before their election, and lay delegates must have been members of The United Methodist Church for at least two years but active participants for at least four years. There is one small but interesting difference in qualifications for lay and ministerial delegates: a minister, to be eligible, must be a full member of the electing conference *when elected* and at the time of the holding of the General and Jurisdictional or Central Conferences to which he or she has been elected. A layperson to be eligible need not be a member within the Annual Conference *when elected*, as long as he or she is a member there at the time of the holding of the General and Jurisdictional or Central Conferences.

Thus, it would be possible for the lay members of an Annual Conference to elect as one of their lay delegates to General Conference a layperson who lived three thousand miles away from his or her conference at the time of the election (as could happen in the case of a nationally prominent layperson who had announced plans to move to the conference in question at a later date) as long as the delegate then became a member of a local church within the Annual Conference prior to the actual time of the holding of the General or Jurisdictional or Central Conference. The ministers could not, under the Constitution, do the same thing, because the minister, to be eligible, must be a member in full connection in that conference *when elected*.

Perhaps the difference here is intended to relieve any episcopal embarrassment which might result if ministers in a conference started voting for a minister they had heard via the grapevine was to be transferred into their conference before any actual transfer had been announced. But the practical effect of the dual requirement of ministers here is that the minister whose conference membership is transferred between the Annual Conference sessions where elections are held and the meeting of the General Conference is ruled out of participating in that General Conference.

The manner of selecting superintendents was one of the key points at issue during the time of negotiations on the Plan of Union, with the E.U.B.'s feeling strongly about the value of electing their superintendents and the Methodists feeling equally strongly about the value of superintendents being under the appointment of the bishop. The decision was finally made that the district superintendency would be an appointive office, but by legislative rather than constitutional provision, so that this could be changed by the General Conference at a later time.

BOUNDARIES. Paragraphs 40-44 deal with technical matters of boundaries and related concerns. Paragraph 40 names the states which make up the five jurisdictions. While Canadian provinces were included in the jurisdictions as established at the 1968 Uniting Conference, a constitutional amendment was shortly adopted which eliminated all Annual Conferences outside the United States from the jurisdictional system.

An interesting constitutional question is raised by Paragraph 42. It indicates that changes in the name, number, or boundaries of Jurisdictional Conferences can be made by the General Conference if it has the consent of the majority of the Annual Conferences of each jurisdiction involved. But, Paragraph 40 gives *constitutional* status to the boundaries of the Jurisdictional Conferences, and would seem to indicate that a constitutional amendment is necessary to change the boundaries. Is Paragraph 42 an alternate method of amending the Constitution as it applies to jurisdictional boundaries, or does Paragraph 62 give the only method of amending the Constitution? If the latter is true, then a two-thirds vote of all the members of all the Annual Conferences would also be necessary. We gladly leave the decision on this matter up to the Judicial Council, should it ever come up.

DISTRICT AND CHARGE CONFERENCES. Paragraph 45 is permissive legislation, under which an Annual Conference may organize District Conferences under appropriate legislation of the General Conference (Pars. 746-748). Paragraphs 46 and 47 give constitutional status to the Charge Conference to be organized in each pastoral charge according to provisions adopted by the General Conference (Pars. 246-251).

EPISCOPAL SUPERVISION. Paragraphs 48-57 provide the constitutional basis of our episcopal form of government. Paragraph 48 makes it clear that the episcopacy of The United Methodist

Church is a continuance of the episcopacy of The Methodist Church and the Evangelical United Brethren Church, and that it is now unified. Constitutional status is given to the Council of Bishops by Paragraph 50, which indicates that the Council shall be made up of all United Methodist bishops, shall meet at least once a year to plan for general oversight and promotion of "temporal and spiritual interests" of the church, and shall carry into effect rules, regulations, and responsibilities set forth by the General Conference and the Plan of Union. The grouping of all the bishops within each Jurisdictional or Central Conference is called the College of Bishops, established in Paragraph 51.

Bishops are appointed to serve within the jurisdiction in which they are elected, but Paragraph 52 gives an elaborate method by which a bishop may be transferred to another jurisdiction. It has never been used yet, and seems rather unlikely to be. The first big hurdles are the bishops themselves, who would undoubtedly really have to want to transfer. How do they communicate this desire to the parties in another jurisdiction without running the risk of making their positions untenable where they are? And if they do communicate it, how likely is it that these parties are going to be successful in persuading all the members of their Jurisdictional Conference to transfer in a bishop to fill a vacancy instead of having their own election to fill the vacancy? And if it should happen that the bishop in question is so popular that the receiving jurisdiction *does* vote to receive him or her, how willing is the present jurisdiction going to be to release that person? It would seem that the most likely case for a transfer to be possible would be where two bishops agreed that they would like to trade jurisdictions. Such a mutual desire might pave the way for a two-way transfer, if there were not other complicating factors involved. All of this is simply to make it clear that while the Constitution provides a method for transfer of bishops between jurisdictions, a large number of human and political dynamics make such transfers extremely difficult, with the end result that bishops tend to stay within their jurisdictions throughout their episcopal careers.

However, the Council of Bishops does have the authority to make temporary and emergency assignments of bishops across jurisdictional lines and Central Conference lines, as long as they have the consent of the bishops resident therein.

Paragraph 53 makes clear that all bishops of The Methodist Church and The Evangelical United Brethren Church at the time of union shall be bishops of The United Methodist Church, and that they shall have life tenure, except those elected by Central Conferences, whose tenure is determined by their respective Central Conferences. The issue of life tenure was another on which differences of practice and conviction between the two former churches had to be resolved. The Methodist Church had, by long tradition, practiced life tenure from the beginning; the E.U.B. Church had always elected their bishops for terms, although they almost always continued to reelect them for life. This issue, like that of the appointive district superintendency, was also resolved in favor of the Methodist practice. But unlike the appointive superintendency, which was not given constitutional status, life tenure of bishops was given such status, and it is clearly spelled out in Paragraph 53. The same paragraph also gives constitutional standing to the Committee on Episcopacy of the Jurisdictional Conference, which is established as the body to which bishops are accountable. This committee, made up of one lay delegate and one ministerial delegate from each Annual Conference in the Jurisdiction, provides an important check against possible abuses of power by bishops, and serves as a continual reminder in our Constitution that our episcopacy is constitutional rather than monarchical in nature. Popular misconceptions outside of United Methodism sometimes picture our bishops as wielding some kind of absolute power once they are elected; this is, of course, false. The bishop's one source of real power is in the appointment of clergy. This will be discussed in more detail in a later chapter.

THE JUDICIARY. Like the government of the United States, United Methodism also has its Supreme Court. It is called the Judicial Council, and it has the power to determine the constitutionality of acts of the General Conference, to hear various appeals on questions of law, and to carry out other duties as specified by the

General Conference. One important difference in the way the Judicial Council functions as compared to the way a Supreme Court in civil government usually operates: the Constitution provides for the Judicial Council to report its findings of unconstitutionality back to the General Conference immediately if it is in session. This enables the General Conference to get rulings on proposed legislation from the Judicial Council, and to make the necessary amendments at the same session if the Council rules the legislation unconstitutional. This is an extremely helpful procedure in perfecting important legislation.

The closing paragraphs of the Constitution deal with the procedure for amending it, which basically requires a two-thirds vote of the General Conference and a two-thirds vote of all the members of all the Annual Conferences. The exceptions to that are the first and second Restrictive Rules dealing with doctrine. Amendments to the Constitution may originate either in the Annual Conferences or at the General Conference, and Jurisdictional and Central Conferences may propose amendments as well.

Doctrinal Statements, the General Rules, and Social Principles

Among the important foundations of our church are the official doctrinal statements (Articles of Religion of The Methodist Church, the Confession of Faith of the Evangelical United Brethren Church, included within the context of the 1988 Report of the Commission on Our Theological Task), the General Rules of The United Methodist Church, and the social principles (1988 Statement of Social Principles). But because the subject of this book is the organization and structure of The United Methodist Church, we will not devote as much space to these matters as was devoted to the Constitution.

The Articles of Religion are an abridged version of the Thirty-nine Articles of the Church of England. They have appeared in their present form in Methodist *Disciplines* since 1790, and they represent orthodox, historical, and evangelical

38

Christian belief. They deal with the Trinity and its meaning, the Bible, the nature of man, sin, and the church. They strike a blow at "Romish" doctrines and practices by denying the doctrine of purgatory and the practice of speaking Latin in the service of worship. They define the sacraments as being two, baptism and the Lord's Supper, and deny the validity of other alleged sacraments as well as the doctrine of transubstantiation. They deal with some practical matters, such as indicating that the marriage of ministers is permissible and that rites and ceremonies may differ in different places; that a Christian's property is not held in common with all other Christians; and that a Christian is permitted to take an oath before a magistrate. Early Methodists, perhaps under some suspicion of lingering allegiance to England because of their Wesleyan ties, adopted an extra article (XXIII) in addition to those suggested by Wesley; this made clear the allegiance of the church to the civil government of the United States. "Of the Duty of Christians to the Civil Authority" (page 63) is an interpretive statement adopted by the Uniting Conference to clarify the meaning of Article XXIII to our churches in other lands. While the Articles of Religion are couched in ancient and somewhat quaint language in places, they have nevertheless stood the test of time and still represent our basic doctrinal position.

The Confession of Faith was adopted in 1962 by The Evangelical United Brethren Church, and was based in turn on doctrinal traditions of the Evangelical Church and the Church of the United Brethren in Christ. By and large, the Confession of Faith simply reiterates in slightly different words the basic doctrines contained in the Articles of Religion, although each of the two statements of faith contains matter not found in the other.

Despite our appreciation for these statements and the truth which they represent, we are grateful that the 1988 General Conference adopted overwhelmingly a report from its Commission on Our Theological Task which places both the Articles and the Confession within the context of a continuing theological search bounded only by "Scripture, tradition, experience, and reason." As the work of theologizing continues, we look forward to continued insights into new possibilities of expressing the truths of an ancient faith in ways which communicate with the minds and hearts of contemporary persons.

Regarding the General Rules, there seems to be some ambiguity. In the Constitution (Par. 19) they are referred to as the General Rules of Our United Societies, but in the Foundation Documents (page 74) they are referred to as the General Rules of The Methodist Church, with only a subheading referring to the United Societies. Are these still valid rules of The United Methodist Church, or are they rules of religious societies of an earlier day which we preserve for historic interest only? As I indicated earlier, I do not believe the Rules to be of binding legal or juridical force, even though ministers coming into full connection are still required to agree to abide by them. But a lack of binding legal status does not diminish the importance of the Rules, which reflect the genius and the spirit of early Methodism. The disciplined life of the small group was at its heart, and whatever heritage of discipline we still possess in United Methodism owes much to the General Rules and what they stand for. Present-day United Methodists, often spiritually flabby and undisciplined, would do well to read and study and ponder anew the General Rules.

The last of the foundations upon which our church is built are its social principles. Both of the uniting churches had had long histories of affirming the indivisibility of the gospel and its necessary application to all of life, including the social needs of humankind. In 1972 a new statement of social principles was adopted which replaced the Methodist Social Creed and the Basic Beliefs Regarding Social Issues and Moral Standards of The Evangelical United Brethren Church. The new document spells our the social concern of the church under these categories: The Natural World, The Nurturing Community, The Social Community, The Economic Community, The Political Community, and The World Community. It also includes a short statement entitled "Our Social Creed," which is intended for liturgical use throughout the church. The entire document makes clear the United Methodist conviction that the gospel is by its very nature "social," and must include this dimension if it is to be true to its Lord.

Finally, any discussion of the foundations of The United Methodist Church would be incomplete without mention of its *Book of Discipline*, or as it is usually called, the *Discipline*. If United Methodism has a unique contribution to make to the Consultation on Church Union or other future church union efforts, it may be at this point. Leaders of other denominations are often fascinated by this book and the contribution it makes to a sense of order and purpose within a far-flung denomination. The denominations will bring varieties of gifts to future unions, but one of United Methodism's unique gifts will surely be its accumulated structural wisdom as contained in its *Book of Discipline*.

Chapter II

THE MINISTRY OF ALL CHRISTIANS

The last half of the twentieth century has seen the rapid growth of a concept of ministry somewhat different from the concept generally held earlier. This emerging concept is one which sees all Christians as being called to ministry, and is a reaction against the tendency in the churches to regard the minister as the person that laypeople hire to do their ministry for them.

The changing concepts of the meaning of ministry, while having a great deal of significance, have also been confusing at times to many within the church. As a result, the 1976 General Conference wrote an entire new chapter into *The Book of Discipline* (Pars. 101-112) which is an attempt to sort out and make clear at the very beginning of the *Discipline* the meaning of this ministry. The opening paragraphs are theological in nature, describing the gift of love which God has made to the world in Christ and the way in which this love takes the form of servant-hood. The ministry of Christ is then seen as a response to that love, and the church as a new covenant which has been made in Christ and in response to the love of God which has been revealed in Christ. This is a general ministry which is required of all Christian believers and is regarded as both a gift and a task. This makes it very clear that every Christian, every believer, is indeed a minister of Jesus Christ.

Within this general ministry there are certain special ministries to which persons may be called. The first of these is the diaconal ministry which is described as a ministry of "love, justice, and service" Persons are to be consecrated as members of the diaconal ministry, and are to remain laypersons within the church. The diaconal ministry, which will be discussed later in this book, is intended to provide recognition of qualified lay professional workers within the church, who serve it in a variety of ways. It should be clear that persons who enter the diaconal ministry do not thereby leave the general ministry but continue to be a part of it.

This chapter of the *Discipline* then goes on to spell out the fact that within the general ministry there are those who are called to specialized ministries of word, sacrament, and order, known as the ordained clergy. These are persons who have evidenced certain gifts and graces and promises of usefulness and devote themselves wholly to the work of the church and to the upbuilding of the general ministry. It is made clear here that the call to the ordained ministry comes inwardly from God and is outwardly affirmed through the judgment and the validation of the church. In United Methodist structure this takes place through the Board of Ordained Ministry and the ordained ministers in full connection at Annual Conference, who must vote upon ordination and conference membership. Again, persons who enter the ordained ministry do not leave the general ministry, but remain a part of it.

The chapter closes on a note reemphasizing the one ministry in Christ and the fact that various parts of that ministry do not rank above other parts. A new paragraph, 113, was added by the 1984 General Conference in an attempt to make clear that The United Methodist Church is not a jural entity capable of being sued.

With this general understanding of the meaning of ministry made clear, we are then ready to move in our *Book of Discipline* into the chapters which describe the actual organization of the structures that are intended to carry out the ministry of Christ in its various forms.

Chapter III

THE LOCAL CHURCH

Definitions

In the first chapter, under the heading "Theological Affirmations," we discussed at some length the United Methodist understanding of the nature of the church. As we now examine the local church, we will not repeat those statements, but seek to amplify and add to them as they apply to the local church.

To the traditional definitions of the local church coming out of the Articles of Religion and Confession of Faith, new understandings have been added. This is especially evident in Paragraph 202:

The Church of Jesus Christ exists in and for the world. It is primarily at the level of the local church that the Church encounters the world. The local church is a strategic base from which Christians move out into the structures of society.

This statement concerning the local church is one which has obviously grown out of new theological views of the church which have been current in recent years, views which see the church not as an institution existing for itself, but as a community whose very reason for existence is to encounter and serve the world in which it lives. This new emphasis is a distinct effort to counteract the tendency toward self-aggrandizement into which it is so easy for

44

institutions, including churches, to fall. This, then, is the image of the servant church, based upon the model of the servanthood of Christ himself, whose continuing body the church is.

The concept of the local church asa base out of which Christians move into the structure of society adds another dimension to traditional definitions of the church. According to this idea, the local church is not so much a place where you go to do church work as it is a training ground from which you go to do your most vital church work in your daily contacts with your fellow workers, your political colleagues, your community organizations, and your family. This view sees the church existing not for itself, but "that the world might be saved." This definition of the local church, taken along with the more traditional definitions, provides a balanced view of the local church which should constantly remind it that worship which does not eventuate in service to the world is sterile, and that service to the world which is not rooted in worship has no lasting foundation.

The concept of the church existing for the world should not be construed, however, as meaning that the local church does not have a special obligation to its own members and those who choose it as their church. This is clearly indicated in Paragraph 204.

The term "pastoral charge" carries certain overtones of meaning in United Methodism. It represents a community of persons over whom a pastor, appointed by a bishop, is *charged* with pastoral oversight. This pastoral charge often consists of one local church, but it may consist of two or more local churches, in which case it is referred to as a "circuit." The term "pastoral charge" also carries a meaning that the pastor is *in charge*. As we will point out later in this chapter, this does not mean that the pastor has the authority to run the church and do all the decision-making. What it does mean is that under the United Methodist system, the pastor appointed to a pastoral charge is held responsible ultimately for what happens in the charge committed to him or her by appointment of the bishop, and should gladly shoulder that responsibility. It is a task which calls for the highest order of strong and sensitive leadership. It is highly unseemly for pastors of The United Methodist Church to be blaming the problems in their church on anyone else but themselves. We who are pastors gladly accept the high honor that goes with being named the pastor of a United Methodist church; we need to be willing to accept the responsibility that goes with it. One of the growing concepts of recent years has been that of the parish, in which a number of local churches, not necessarily United Methodist, come together to provide various forms of ministry to a certain area. There is widespread use of the parish idea in urban areas, as churches come together to meet the needs of the inner city, and in rural areas where declining populations often call for new forms of organization to meet the needs of people. The parish concept is also a recognition of the growing need for specialized ministries, which a grouping of churches and ministers may make possible, even as group medical practice meets needs of people which the general practitioner is increasingly unable to meet. Paragraph 206 gives disciplinary recognition to the parish.

The Meaning of Church Membership

To be a member of a local United Methodist church is to be a member of the total United Methodist connection (Par. 210) and a member of the Church Universal (Par. 208). This means that becoming a member of the church means becoming a member of a fellowship without boundaries of time or geography, a fellowship extending around the world and through the centuries of history, a fellowship made up of those who call Jesus Christ "Lord" and who come together to carry out his purpose in the world. Every local church, then, everywhere, is open to all persons, regardless of race, color, national origin, or economic condition, when they take the appropriate vows of membership.

These vows are considered to be a kind of covenant with God and with the members of the local church, and they are made in response to five basic questions, which are asked of all persons seeking membership, in the presence of the congregation. The questions are as follows:

Do you here, in the presence of God, and of this congregation, renew the solemn promise and vow that you made, or that was made in your name, at your Baptism?

This question assumes, then, that all persons seeking membership have been baptized, for this is considered the essential first step into the community of believers. The question recognizes that the baptismal vows may have been taken for them by their parents, perhaps when they were infants. These persons are now confirming for themselves an act which was done by others on their behalf years before; or they may simply be reaffirming vows of baptism which they themselves spoke only a few minutes before as a part of the same worship service in which they are now being confirmed. Either way, this vow is a recognition of the historic two-step procedure toward becoming a full member of the church: baptism and confirmation.

Do you confess Jesus Christ as your Lord and Savior and pledge your allegiance to his kingdom?

This confession, or declaration of belief, is central to the matter of being a Christian. It is much more than simply a theoretical and philosophical affirmation of a doctrine; it is a personal pledge of loyalty to Jesus Christ and all for which he stands. Someone has said that when persons are challenged as to why they are Christian, they do not so much make an argument as point to a person. That is, a Christian is defined more in terms of following Christ than in terms of having a particular doctrine or theory *about* Christ. Theories may differ, but the Christ we follow remains the same.

Do you receive and profess the Christian faith as contained in the Scriptures of the Old and New Testaments?

This question is important because it clearly identifies the Christian faith with the biblical faith. A so-called Christian faith unrelated to the revelation of the Old and New Testaments is a contradiction in terms. However, the interpretation of this biblical Christian faith is not spelled out, for according to the Protestant doctrine of the priesthood of all believers every Christian is free to read and interpret the Bible for himself or herself. Because United Methodists believe passionately in this kind of freedom, there exist

47

wide diversities of interpretation of the Christian faith within our fellowship. This diversity in unity is something in which we rejoice.

Do you promise according to the grace given you to live a Christian life and always remain a faithful member of Christ's holy Church?

Up until this question, the queries have been doctrinal in nature. Now this question moves to a practical level, and calls for everyday deeds and attitudes which will reflect the doctrinal affirmations already made. Are the words "according to the grace given you" a sort of loophole which can later justify members' doing almost anything they please? Not if we understand the Wesleyan idea of grace, which is seen as free, being poured out abundantly on all persons, and enabling them to accept the gifts of salvation. So, far from providing an excuse for possible later failures, this phrase provides rather the source of the motivation which enables us to promise to live a Christian life. It is life lived in grateful response to God's gracious gift in Christ.

It is at this point in the ritual, after affirmative answers have been given to the four questions above, that new members are actually confirmed. It is important to note that up to and through the actual confirmation, there is no mention of The United Methodist Church. The persons are being received into the Church of God, confirmed in the "faith and fellowship of all true disciples of Jesus Christ." This is the central and truly important fact of confirmation.

It is only after the actual confirmation that those who have been confirmed, joined by others who have been members of other communions (denominations) who now wish to unite with this local church, are asked another question:

Will you be loyal to The United Methodist Church, and uphold it by your prayers, your presence, your gifts, and your service?

This question pins down specific responsibility toward that branch of Christ's Church with which they are now uniting:

namely, The United Methodist Church. It is a clear recognition of the fact that membership in the church involves a two-way street of both privileges and responsibilities. If the church is "people in mission," then the people must assume responsibility for the carrying out of that mission. Furthermore, this last question does not assume permanent membership in The United Methodist Church. A person contemplating church membership once asked about this question, "Does this mean I am bound to be a Methodist all my life, even if I move to a community where there is no United Methodist church within reasonable distance?" The answer to that question is no. The church you are joining and of which you promise to be a faithful member all the days of your life is the Church of God, or the Church of Jesus Christ. Your promise of loyalty to The United Methodist Church is no less serious and may well involve a lifetime of loyalty to that branch of Christ's Church, but by its own definitions The United Methodist Church has no right to lay such claims upon its members—to do so would be contrary to its own view of itself set forth in Paragraph 203 of the *Discipline*. So it is perfectly proper for you to undertake this last vow, understanding that it is in effect until such time as your own circumstances may dictate that you should transfer your membership to a church of another denomination. So, we join the Church of Jesus Christ for good; we join the United Methodist branch of that church *maybe* for good, but in the increasingly mobile society of which we are a part, quite likely it is for the time being, as families move into communities which may be served by other branches of the church.

A technical definition of the membership of a local United Methodist church is given in Paragraph 209, indicating that it shall include "all baptized persons who have come into membership by confession of faith or transfer and whose names have not been removed from the membership rolls by reason of death, transfer, withdrawal, or removal for cause."

While membership in The United Methodist Church is open to all who are prepared to take the vows, it is assumed that such persons will undergo a period of instruction and training first. The exact length and extent of this training is not spelled out, other than being a "reasonable period" (Par. 216.I). Most pastors would insist on at least a four-session training period for adults, with many pastors feeling that a considerably longer period is called for. Certainly the presence on our church rolls of large numbers of nominal members who seem to possess little knowledge of what it means to be a Christian and a part of the Christian Church would indicate that much more stress must be placed on thorough grounding of potential members in the Christian faith. They must really understand what it means to be a Christian, especially in preparation for times when being a Christian may not be easy.

In the matter of membership training for children, the pastor carries special responsibilities, even though it is recognized that preparation is going on all through the child's church school experience. The age for confirmation is not specified, but it is spelled out that children completing the sixth grade shall normally be the youngest recruited for confirmation preparation. However, if children at a younger age seek to be enrolled of their own volition, the pastor may, at his or her discretion, accept them. There is no unanimity of opinion among pastors as to the proper age for confirmation training, but a considerable number feel that it should be several years past the minimal sixth-grade disciplinary requirement, on the ground that more mature children will better understand and remember their training. Other pastors defend giving the training at the sixth-grade level, on the ground that if you wait much longer, the children may not be around. So the debate continues, and there will continue to be some variation in these matters from church to church, depending upon the pastor and his or her particular philosophy.

But the *Discipline* does establish a norm for a minimum age to bring children into confirmation classes: "youth who, are completing the sixth grade." The number of sessions of the classes again may vary greatly, with most pastors wanting a minimum of ten or twelve weeks, but with others establishing a confirmation program which may extend over one or two years. Always the main concern is for those to be confirmed to know what they are getting into, so that church membership is not merely a formality, a nice convention, or "the thing to do." During the period of preparation those in the class are to be enrolled as "preparatory members," along with all baptized children who have not yet become full members (Par. 216.4) and youth of the church eighteen years or younger (Par. 232.2).

Ordinarily, persons joining the church do so in the presence of the congregation. However, the pastor may, at his or her discretion, receive a person who is unable to be present before the congregation. This should certainly be done sparingly, for much of the meaning of confirmation is found in the participation of the congregation, and it should never be done simply for someone's convenience. There are a few other cases where a person may join a congregation without appearing before it, and chaplains are authorized to receive persons into the membership of The United Methodist Church and then send notice of this to the local congregation involved (Par. 217). Another interesting provision of this same paragraph permits duly authorized ministers of The United Methodist Church, if they are "otherwise present where a local church is not available," to receive such persons into membership after they have taken the vows, and then enroll them in the local church of their choice. Presumably, under this paragraph a United Methodist minister from California vacationing in Alaska could receive a hunting guide into the membership of the church, if requested by the guide. And if the guide lived where a local church was not available and if the guide so requested, the minister could enroll him or her in a local church in New York City. Such are the benefits of the connectional system!

Persons who are members in good standing of other Christian denominations, and have been baptized, may be received into the church by certificate of transfer; or, if they have been members of churches which do not issue such certificates, they may be received on their declaration of faith and their willingness to be loyal to The United Methodist Church.

Two special categories of membership are provided for persons who are residing for an extended period of time away from their home church, and wish to be associated with the church of their temporary residence. If the persons in question are United Methodists, they may be enrolled in the church where they temporarily reside as affiliate members, which qualifies them to participate and hold office where they are, although they will still be counted as members in their home churches. A person in the same situation, whose home church is of another denomination, may be enrolled as an associate member with the same privileges.

The United Methodist Church recognizes that in addition to receiving members into the fellowship it has a responsibility to help them faithfully perform their vows and successfully live the Christian life. Individual members do carry a "primary responsibility" here (Par. 230), but the local church through its pastor and Council on Ministries is expected to provide a program of care and nurture through small groups, visitation, and other means which will assure the members of the continuing care and concern of the church (Pars. 228-230).

TRANSFER OR TERMINATION OF MEMBERSHIP. There are basically five ways in which membership in a local United Methodist church can be terminated: by death, transfer, withdrawal, expulsion, or action of the Charge Conference (Pars. 236-243).

Death would seem to need no explanation, although sometimes deceased persons are carried on the rolls for years; one is uncertain as to why this happens—whether a pastor is concerned with keeping the statistics looking good or whether in the case of some members the pastor doesn't notice they're dead. At any rate, death is supposed to terminate membership.

Transfer is simply a way of changing the locus of membership from one local church to another, either United Methodist or another denomination. The *Discipline* makes clear the duty of all pastors to do everything in their power to see that transfers are effected so that persons become members where they are, including notifying the pastor of the church in the community where the person resides. If they do not know who the pastor is, they should notify the district superintendent that the member has moved; and if they do not know who the district superintendent is, they should send the name and address to the General Board of Discipleship. These duties are often not carried out too faithfully in local churches, with the result that many of them carry on their rolls year after year a large number of nonresident members. This is not a healthy situation, and pastors and Councils on Ministries need to take the broad view and make a real effort to follow the *Discipline* at this point and get people related to local churches where they live. Every local church doing this faithfully could help revitalize the whole church, especially in a period of increasing mobility of families.

Withdrawal, as its name implies, is the voluntary giving up of membership. It must be communicated in writing to the pastor, who shall then put in the records that the person has "withdrawn." In the case (which happens quite frequently) of a person who has united with another denomination without notice, the pastor shall confirm this, and then enter "withdrawn" on the records.

Expulsion is so rarely used that it hardly needs to be mentioned, but involves members tried under the church trial procedures of the *Discipline* and expelled.

"Action of the Charge Conference" is the last means of terminating membership in the local church. It is an action which may be taken only after members have stopped participating in any way in the life of the church, and efforts have been made by the church over a period of three years to locate and reactivate them (or if their address is unknown). In addition, the name of the person must be entered in the Charge Conference minutes for three consecutive years before the action can be taken. Only then can the Charge Conference, on recommendation of the pastor and the evangelism work area chairperson, remove the name. Each name must be considered individually by the Charge Conference. All these precautions are important because we believe church membership is important and should not be terminated lightly. On the other hand, our heritage and beginnings as a disciplined society convince us that membership carries with it obligations which are the responsibility of the individual, and that there is a certain dishonesty in carrying people as members who have long since refused to accept any responsibility.

So the above are the five methods by which a person's membership in a local church may be transferred or terminated. It should be emphasized that in no case do pastors have any power to terminate or transfer membership simply by their own action. Sometimes pastors will simply cross out the names of members who have been inactive or whom they don't know. Such practices are an unconscionable violation of every concept of due process, and treat church membership with a disregard which is surely unbecoming to the Christian Church. Here is one place where careful observance of the provisions of the *Discipline* is essential, if we are to minister to people with due regard to their status and dignity as children of God and members of the Christian community.

How New Churches Are Started

Reading the paragraph in the *Discipline* related to organizing new local churches (Par. 270) might give a stranger a distorted picture. The *Discipline* seems to show the bishop and his cabinet studying a map of the conference, giving consideration to the conference Board of Global Ministries' program for home missions and church extension, and then the bishop saying, "We are going to organize a church in X District." The language of the *Discipline* would then indicate that the district superintendent takes it from there and makes recommendations to the district Board of Church Location and Building and to the city or district missionary society on a place to start the new congregation. After these bodies have acted favorably, the superintendent proceeds with the work of organizing the congregation.

The only trouble with this description is that this isn't the way most new congregations get started. They actually get started by a need for a congregation becoming evident in a particular locality, *and* a district superintendent seeing that need and carrying the ball to see that it is met. The need may become evident to the superintendent in a number of ways: one of the pastors may call attention to a new community that is filled with people and lacks adequate church coverage; a small group of laypersons in the new community may come to the superintendent with a request for the services of the church; in some areas the superintendent may be requested by a council of churches, as a result of surveys they have made, to take responsibility for a certain place; or a local church may feel a responsibility for a certain area which could be better served by a newly established local church. The district superintendent then becomes the key person in taking this need through channels in order to make the idea become a reality. Thus, the provisions of Paragraph 270.1 begin to make sense when it is realized that they describe a "screening process" in the starting of new churches, and not the real initiatory process. This screening process is necessary in order to ensure that commitments to start new churches do not overtax the personnel and financial resources of the conference.

So what really happens in the starting of a new church is that a district superintendent who has become convinced of the need for a new church in a particular location takes the case to the bishop and the cabinet. It may be that several other superintendents also have pressing needs to start new churches. Is there enough ministerial personnel available in the conference so that an able person can be placed in the field to be the pastor? If personnel is limited, which of the pressing needs is most pressing? These are some of the questions the bishop and his/her cabinet must answer. Then they must confer with the conference Board of Global Ministries because this body is the one which holds the purse strings for money for the project—both for salary for the new pastor and grant and loan money for the purchase of land and erection of buildings. The *Discipline* provides only that the Board of Global Ministries must give due consideration to the project, not that they must approve of it. Theoretically, then, the bishop and his cabinet could proceed to establish a new congregation even though the Board of Global Ministries was opposed to the project; however, the superintendent might have real difficulties later when he or she came to the board requesting funds for the project. So, as a practical matter, the provisions of Paragraph 270.1 are designed to ensure that before a new congregation is started, the bodies who must provide the resources of personnel (the bishop and his/her cabinet) and of money (the conference Board of Global Ministries) support the project.

After the approval of the bishop has been secured, the superintendent must get the approval of the district Board of

Church Location and Building (Par. 2518) and (where there is one) the city or district mission structure (Par. 1415.7). Again, as a practical matter, the superintendent will undoubtedly have counseled with those bodies long before this in order to get their local reaction to the project before presenting it to the bishop and his/her cabinet for consideration.

The actual constituting of the new local church does not take place usually until some months after a pastor has been appointed to the field, has commenced holding services, and has gathered the nucleus of a congregation together. The only person who can actually constitute a new local church is the district superintendent or the pastor who has been given specific authority to do so by the superintendent.

On the appointed day (usually on a Sunday after worship), those who desire to unite with the church are invited to present themselves for membership, by transfer and by profession of faith. The appointed pastor after working with this group for some weeks has prepared them for this step. As soon as these persons have been received, the superintendent immediately convenes the Constituting Church Conference, made up of all the members just received, all of whom are entitled to vote. This conference has only one duty: to elect members at large. Once they are elected, the presiding officer declares the church properly constituted. He or she then adjourns the Constituting Conference and calls the Charge Conference into session, which is composed of all the people just elected, plus any ex-officio members as provided in the *Discipline*. This conference then proceeds to elect the necessary officers, trustees, and committees necessary to operate a church.

For persons who have had the privilege of being part of starting a new local church, it is an unforgettable experience. Like any birth of a new being, it is full of excitement and hope for the future.

One encouraging development in the starting of new churches is the growing ecumenical involvement in the process. In many areas new churches are not begun without clearance with the council of churches, in order to avoid the costly "over-churching" of areas which has often plagued us in the past. Not only this, but in some places two or more denominations are joining in the sponsoring of a new church, with an agreement that the church shall actually be under the administration of one of them. This procedure makes possible extra resources for land and buildings which are often necessary in the beginning of a new church, but avoids the pitfalls of "federation" by having the church administered by only one denomination. Certainly the future calls for more and more ecumenical involvement in the important matter of beginning new congregations.

How Churches Are Governed

Though the pastor of the charge (one or more churches) appointed by the bishop is to be "in charge," the actual policies and programs of the local church are made by democratically elected bodies and officials, operating within the framework provided in the *Discipline*. On the other hand, this does not mean that the pastor is expected simply to be an executive secretary whose role is to carry out the decisions of the governing bodies. Rather, the pastor is expected to be involved creatively in the decision-making process, feeling free to initiate ideas without dominating the scene. Thus, this is a delicate role which requires imagination, a lack of defensiveness about one's own ideas when they are not accepted, an enthusiasm for good ideas presented by others, and most important of all, a genuine Christian love for people, which encourages the group process and results in sound plans and programs. This effort is especially important for a pastor, because the role of preacher and priest surround a pastor with a certain mystique which can sometimes silence laypeople reluctant to disagree with him or her publicly. An example of this attitude can be seen in the half-facetious remark of a veteran layman who said that he believed that if the pastor got up in the board meeting and moved that they burn down the church, someone would second it and it would pass unanimously! Actually, the structures of the local church provides quite adequately for genuine participatory democracy; what is needed is for ministers and laity to try much harder than they have to make it work.

THE CHARGE CONFERENCE. The supreme governing body in the affairs of the local church is the Charge Conference. It is not only

57

the connecting link between the local church and The United Methodist Church as a whole, but it has general oversight of the Administrative Board, which is the continuing year-round governing body. While historically the Charge Conference met quarterly and filled an important ongoing place in the life of the local church, in United Methodism the image of the Charge Conference becomes more and more that of an annual meeting. It may be called into special session on other occasions, usually related to taking action on important property matters which require Charge Conference approval.

The membership of the Charge Conference is identical with that of the Administrative Board, with the exception that retired ministers who elect to hold their membership in a Charge Conference do not thereby become members of the Administrative Board. Two questions which may then be asked with some logic are: "If the membership of the Charge Conference and the Administrative Board is practically identical, why then separate them into two bodies? Why the administrative superstructure?" The answer to these questions centers almost entirely in the presence or absence of one person: the district superintendent. Certain key decisions and actions of the local church can be made only by the Charge Conference. The district superintendent must either call or give written consent to the pastor to call a Charge Conference and preside over it unless an elder has been designated by the district superintendent to preside in his or her place. The importance of this provision to the connectional system cannot be overstressed. It means that no local church can make the decisions most important to its life in isolation from the whole church as personified in the district superintendent, whose very presence in the presiding officer's chair is a containing reminder that each local church is a part of a larger whole. Thus, the structure of the Charge Conference is a way of guaranteeing the presence of that representative of The United Methodist Church, the district superintendent, at least annually and at other times of crucial decision-making in the local church. So, while the district superintendent may authorize an elder to preside, this should be invoked only in rare instances and only when absolutely necessary.

As we have indicated, the membership of the Charge Conference is practically identical with that of the Administrative Board. Each is made up of the major elected officers of the church, chairpersons of work areas, chairpersons of certain key committees, presidents of United Methodist Women and United Methodist Men, and members at large. The pastor and other employed professional staff are also members (Par. 246). In addition, retired ministers who elect to hold their Charge Conference membership therein are also members. Paragraph 246.2 also includes "others as may be designated in the *Discipline.*" Whom does this include? It would definitely include local pastors. It would also appear that ministers on leave of absence (Par. 448) and honorably or administratively located ministers (Pars. 452.1 and 453.3) also have membership in a Charge Conference, although the language is a bit ambiguous. Ministers under special appointment also have membership in a Charge Conference of their choice within the bounds of the Annual Conference (Par. 443.3).

One of the weak points in our structure is that, basically, the members of the Charge Conference are elected by themselves. While in actual practice this may present no problem, it certainly does open the door for a self-perpetuating power structure within the local church. An optional procedure which avoids this structural defect is provided in Paragraph 248, where the functions of the Charge Conference may be carried out by the Church Conference, consisting of all the members of the local church. This may be authorized by the district superintendent on written request of the pastor or Administrative Board, or of 10 percent of the local church membership, or simply at the discretion of the district superintendent. In the discussions of the Plan of Union, the term "Congregational Meeting" was first proposed, but this raised fears among some that this might be construed as a retreat from connectionalism; hence the term "Annual Church Conference," later amended to "Church Conference," was agreed upon.

This provision is being widely used throughout United Methodism, and would seem to provide a healthy opportunity for every member of the local church to have some sense of participation in its government. It also, however, provides an opportunity for a determined minority to pack a meeting much more readily than would be the case in the Charge Conference. This is undoubtedly one of the reasons why the Church Conference has not become a mandatory structure for the local church, but is optional, subject to the approval of the district superintendent. However, the interests of genuine participatory democracy seem to indicate that future General Conferences might well consider making the Church Conference a standard part of the structure of the local church. Certainly the election of the members of the Charge Conference should be done by a body other than the Charge Conference itself.

One of the interesting features of the Charge Conference, which applies also to the Administrative Board, is the provision for a quorum. "The members present and voting at any duly announced meeting shall constitute a quorum" (Par. 246.6). This is a provision drastically different from most organizations, which usually require a stated number of persons to be present for a quorum. But United Methodism by long tradition has refused to let its structure be immobilized by members staying home, either deliberately or through apathy. Thus, if a Charge Conference has been properly called with ten days' notice, and only the district superintendent and one other person show up for the meeting, the business can go forward. (If the superintendent were a stickler for parliamentary procedure, he or she might require two members to be present, so that there would be someone to second motions!)

Some might quarrel with this rather unusual provision of United Methodist practice, but it does have the healthy effect of letting people know that no Charge Conference or Administrative Board meeting is going to be kept from acting by technical provisions of lack of a quorum, and that they had better be there if they want to help shape the decisions of the church. It avoids the deadly situation where members can stymie action simply by staying away.

The powers and duties of the Charge Conference are spelled out in Paragraph 247. This supreme governing body of the local church has the task of hearing reports of the officers and committees and organizations of the church, evaluating the effectiveness of the total program, and establishing goals and proposals to be implemented by the Administration Board. It has the task of electing all the important officers and committees of the church. It stands in an awesome place of responsibility with regard to candidates for the ministry, for it must give its recommendation (by written ballot with a two-thirds majority) to all candidates for the ministry from the local church before they can qualify. The intent of the provision is to be sure that the people who know the candidates best really believe that they have the "gifts and graces" to be good ministers of Jesus Christ. This is a profoundly serious responsibility, and the tendency of churches to sometimes treat this as a mere formality has often led to the tragic results of persons entering the ministry who were never suited for it.

Two of the most important areas of concern of the Charge Conference are the setting of the pastor's salary for the year ahead and the interpretation of the amount the church has been apportioned for World Service and conference benevolences. There are several reasons why these items are reserved for Charge Conference consideration when the district superintendent is present. First, the superintendent has a special concern that the ministers under his or her jurisdiction are receiving adequate support. Laypersons are also usually sensitive to this need, but in case they are not, many ministers (not all, by any means) may feel reluctant about pressing for an increase in their own salary. So the superintendent becomes their advocate, and may lay upon the Charge Conference's conscience the need to do something about their pastor's salary. The Charge Conference is not likely to take the superintendent's words lightly, because they know that he or she has a key role in making the appointments of the ministers, including their minister, and that if they are not willing to provide adequate pastoral support, there are other churches that are. Thus, the district superintendent is in a unique position to do extremely effective work on behalf of better salaries for ministers, and the Charge Conference is one of the places to do this.

A second reason why these two financial matters are special concerns of the Charge Conference is somewhat opposite from the first. That is, sometimes a local church will decide it wants to give a big raise to its pastor, but it is going to do this by not paying its share of the World Service and conference benevolence budget. Here again the district superintendent becomes an advocate, but this time for all the missionaries and workers of our church who must depend upon the faithfulness of the local churches to sustain them. These servants of God are literally at the mercy of the members of the Charge Conferences in the matter of their financial support; the district superintendent becomes their spokesperson, and reminds the Charge Conference of the inequity involved in raising the salary of one of their workers (their pastor) while at the same time cutting their support of their other workers (their missionaries and other conference and national personnel).

The extent to which district superintendents succeed in this effort will depend upon how much trust the members of the Charge Conference place in them, for their arguments are based on moral force and not on disciplinary sanctions. For the average member of the average Charge Conference, the district superintendent personifies The United Methodist Church; if they trust him or her they tend to trust the church. This is one of the reasons why the role of district superintendent is more crucial to the ongoing work of connectional United Methodism than any other, and why their presence as presiding officers of the local Charge Conference is so fundamental to our polity.

Thus, the structure of the Charge Conference in the local church becomes understandable when we realize that it is simply a means to ensure that the most important decisions that the church makes are not made in isolation from the whole church. While the presence of the district superintendent does not dictate the decisions to be made, it does provide that they shall be made in the light of the total responsibility which a local United Methodist church carries.

THE ADMINISTRATIVE BOARD. While the supreme governing body of the local church is the Charge Conference, the most important month-to-month governing body is the Administrative Board. As indicated previously, it is made up of essentially the same personnel as the Charge Conference, but the district superintendent does not preside. The number of persons on the board will vary according to the size of the local church. Certain officers are members of the board by virtue of their office in the church, but there is a provision for the election of members at large (Par. 254). Thus, in quite large churches it would not be unusual for the board to have a hundred or more members, while in a small church there might be fifteen. The board is elected by the Charge Conference, and is amenable to it. In turn, all members, organizations, and agencies of the local church are amenable to the Administrative Board, except the trustees, who are amenable to the Charge Conference. So it occupies a key place in the local church structure.

The *Discipline* requires the board to meet at least quarterly. This is a minimal meeting requirement, and in many local churches monthly meetings of the Administrative Board are the practice. This is especially true in larger churches where the idea of involving as many people as possible in regular decision-making is felt to be important.

The officers of the board are chairperson, vice-chairperson, and recording secretary, all of whom are to be laypersons nominated by the Nominating Committee or from the floor and elected by the board.

The board has "general oversight of the administration and program of the local church" (Par. 253.1). The pastor serves as the administrative officer and as such is an ex-officio member of all the official groups in the church. "Ex officio" is one of those vague terms which simply means "by reason of office" and says nothing about whether the pastor has a vote or not. Practices undoubtedly differ from pastor to pastor, but most pastors probably feel that having a voice in all the various commissions and committees is quite sufficient without also exercising a vote in all of them. While this ex-officio membership ordinarily gives the pastor the right to be present at any group meeting, there is one important exception to this: the Pastor-Parish Relations Committee may meet with the district superintendent without the minister being present under certain conditions (Par. 269.2e). This is a logical exception, since such a meeting would not be concerned with the program of the local church but rather with the pastor's own status. The privilege of meeting in such executive session is the indispensable prerogative of any group charged with the supervision of personnel.

In addition to broad responsibilities of programming and goal setting, the board has certain fiscal responsibilities which are important, primarily in the adoption of the budget. While the Committee on Finance has the responsibility of bringing together all financial askings for the year and recommending a budget, it is the board which has final authority, and it may change the budget as it sees fit. Since the Committee on Finance also has the responsibility of implementing the plans for raising the money for the budget, the board had better be ready, if it votes to add items to the budget as recommended, to give its wholehearted support to going out to raise pledges. To put it more bluntly, it is hardly fair to the Committee on Finance to ask them to bring in a carefully thought-out budget, then have the board add a considerable amount to it and dump it back in the lap of the Committee on Finance to raise. Whether the board adds to the budget or not, it needs to assume responsibility for the budget it has voted and give every effort to see that it is underwritten. This will undoubtedly happen if the members of the board are the kind of persons whom the *Discipline* expects them to be, "persons of genuine Christian character who love the Church, are morally disciplined, are committed to the mandate of inclusiveness in the life of the church, are loyal to the ethical standards of The United Methodist Church set forth in the Social Principles, and are competent to administer its affairs" (Par. 254).

Some of the officers who are members of the board are of such key importance that a brief description of their roles is in order. The lay leader is the top lay official of a local church; often serving as chairperson of the Administrative Board, though not necessarily. Lay leaders should be persons with a broad understanding of the total work of The United Methodist Church which enables them to communicate and counsel with the pastor. This is very important, because one of the problems of the pastor is that almost all laypersons in the official family of the church have a special interest; that is, they are concerned with a specific area of the church's life in which they carry responsibility, and quite naturally so. But this may make it difficult for the layperson to see the importance of other areas of the church life for which the pastor is equally responsible. A lay leader who makes it his or her business to acquire a good understanding of the total work of the church can be of tremendous help to the pastor and a very effective interpreter of the total mission of the church to the members. A warm rapport between lay leader and pastor, based upon mutual respect and loyalty, is essential to the effective functioning of a local church. While it has sometimes been assumed in the past that the lay leader must be a man, this has never been true, and in practice is being increasingly filled by laity of both sexes. A new emergence of the importance of United Methodist Men in the local church gives increased emphasis to the necessity of considering the office of lay leader one relating to the whole membership of the local church, and consequently open to the whole membership.

The lay member (or members) of Annual Conference is another key officer, because this person is the representative of the local church to the Annual Conference and votes on matters which may profoundly affect the local church. Because this office is so important, it needs to be filled by the most highly qualified person available. Because this office involves attendance at Annual Conference for several days or most of a week, the standard for election sometimes becomes, "Who can get away to do this?" This is really tragic, for the church today simply cannot afford to be represented by any other than the most qualified of its lay personnel in important decision-making roles. The lay member needs to be an effective communicator, who can return from the Annual Conference and convey to the local church the significance of Annual Conference actions.

THE COUNCIL ON MINISTRIES. One of the structures created at the Uniting Conference at Dallas is the local church Council on Ministries, which is amenable to the Administrative Board. The council is a small strategy group, made up of key officers, work area chairpersons, age-level coordinators, staff, and youth members. It is envisioned as an "idea" group, constantly studying the local church's strategy for mission, and coming up with new ideas and directions for the church. Once these proposed ideas get the approval of the Administrative Board, it then becomes the council's task to implement them.

Opinion differs within the church as to the exact relationship between the Administrative Board and the Council on Ministries. Many pastors, especially of smaller churches which, before the Plan of Union, often felt burdened down with excessive compulsory administrative machinery, have welcomed the Council on Ministries as a much more realistic and effective way of administering the local church and a way of avoiding what seemed to them an artificial compartmentalization of the work of the church under the commission form. Many of these pastors are relying heavily on the Council on Ministries as a primary administrative vehicle and relegating the Administrative Board to a relatively minor position. On the other hand, many pastors, particularly of larger churches, are continuing to think of the Administrative Board as the primary focus of administration, with meetings being held on a monthly basis, and the Council on Ministries functioning primarily as a coordinating and consultative group. Part of the concern here is to involve as large a number of persons in the decision-making process as possible, and to avoid the situation where a small group makes all the important decisions. Undoubtedly these differences of philosophy will continue to exist within the local churches, with each church establishing its course based on its size, its situation, and the outlook of its ministerial and lay leadership. This is perfectly proper, since one of the marks of local church structure in United Methodism is a new sense of flexibility. In fact, under the provisions of paragraph 247.2 local churches with special needs and tasks can develop almost any form of organization they want, as long as it is approved by the district superintendent and provides for avenues of communication with the connectional church. And legislation of the 1980 General Conference allows smaller churches to combine the Administrative Board and the Council on Ministries in an Administrative Council (Par. 252).

AGE-LEVEL COORDINATORS AND WORK AREA CHAIRPERSONS. Two seemingly conflicting philosophies of carrying out the work of the church seem to be present in these offices. The theory of age-level coordination is that the Council on Ministries develops a program of total ministry and the age-level coordinator then implements and coordinates it within that age level. The theory of the work area is that after the council develops a program of total ministry, the work area chairperson or commission takes responsibility for implementing that portion of it which falls within the scope of interest of that work area, perhaps covering several age levels. In other words, one might be considered a horizontal approach to programming (age level), and one vertical (by interest or function).

I indicated above that these two approaches were seemingly conflicting. They are not inherently conflicting, because the Council on Ministries remains the key group which assigns responsibilities for implementing programs in such a way that conflicts do not arise. This is the theory of the structure, but there is some question as to whether so much responsibility is then laid on the Council on Ministries that it cannot carry the load. It is this concern which has prompted many larger churches to retain a strong Administrative Board and commission system in an effort to spread the work load among more people, with the Council on Ministries serving as a coordinating and consultative group, but without assuming the full responsibilities envisioned in the *Discipline*. As local churches work with the structure and gain experience, there will undoubtedly come changes which will refine and strengthen the structure and resolve what seem to be ambiguities to many local churches and pastors.

One of the helpful programming concepts for the local church is that of the "task groups" (Par. 267), which is a means by which the Council on Ministries can establish a non-permanent group to accomplish certain specific goals in the mission of the church.

COMMITTEES. There are three mandatory committees in the structure of each local church which deserve mention because of their importance.

The Committee on Nominations and Personnel, as its name

implies, has the task of presenting nominations annually (and at other times as needed) for practically all the offices, committees, and commissions of the local church. This committee is elected for three-year terms, staggered so that continuity on the committee will be maintained. One unique feature about this committee is that it does not present nominations to fill vacancies in its own ranks. Rather, such vacancies are filled by nominations from the floor of the Charge Conference. This is designed to ensure that a nominating committee will not have the chance to perpetuate itself or to keep a certain group in this key place if it is not the will of the Charge Conference. The mandatory nominations from the floor provide a sort of safety valve which protects against any such monopolies. Actually, this committee, when it functions properly, has such hard work to do that most people are glad to be relieved of it after three years. While the big part of this committee's work is in preparation for the annual elections, it also has responsibility throughout the year for working with personnel (other than employed staff) in conjunction with the Administrative Board and Council on Ministries.

The pastor is the chairperson of this committee, and thus is in a position to exert considerable influence in the matter of nominations. This is appropriate, since the pastors bear responsibility for the work of the local church. They certainly need a strong voice in naming the persons they must depend on to work with them in the task. The committee needs to recognize this and give careful consideration to the pastor's opinions, but must not be afraid to disagree when they feel he or she is wrong. In the final analysis, the nominations are made by the committee, not the pastor.

The Committee on Pastor-Parish Relations is an extremely important group, since it deals with the delicate matter of the relations between the pastor (and other employed staff) and the people of the church. The whole concept of this committee in the *Discipline* is of a continuing, positive, creative group whose primary function is to aid the pastor (staff) in making his or her ministry effective by being available for counsel, keeping the pastor advised concerning conditions within the congregation as they affect relations between pastor and people, and continually interpreting to the people the nature and function of the pastoral office. The role of this committee is *not* to lie dormant until some kind of crisis develops, and then to meet "to get a new pastor." If the committee is to perform its true function, then, its first requirement is to meet regularly. The *Discipline* provides that it meet at least quarterly; many pastors and laypersons feel that it ought to meet more often. Only by doing this can it develop the rapport with the pastor and the knowledge of the pastoral task which is so important. The committee also needs to remember that it functions as a two-way street; not only to inform the pastor of conditions within the congregation, but to inform the congregation of the nature and functions of the pastoral office. This means, for instance, that the committee will take the lead in informing the congregation of the pastor's need for study time, for continuing education opportunities, and for adequate days off and vacation time. If the committee has failed, then the pastor is left to fend for himself or herself on such matters.

There is certain etiquette and good taste which a pastor needs to observe in the relations with this committee. Pastors should not insist on being present every minute when the committee meets. They should have the good sense to arrive late enough to give the committee a chance to talk among themselves for a while. If they do not do this, they cut off the possibility for the committee to do its work. In other words, they stop up the safety valve. When this happens it ultimately causes explosions. The wise pastor will give the committee a chance to function, and will seek to develop an open and non-defensive attitude and atmosphere where matters of concern can be discussed frankly and growth can take place on all sides. A Pastor-Parish Relations Committee which is really doing its job well can be one of the most exciting Christian growth groups in the church!

It is also true that when all efforts have been made, it may become evident to the committee that the best interests of the charge and the pastor will be served by a change of pastors. The committee is then obliged to furnish the pastor with this information. The committee may be reluctant to do this rather unpleasant duty, and may be tempted simply to tell the superintendent of their desire. But this course has dangers. If the superintendent suggests a move to a pastor who does not want to move, the superintendent is then almost forced to tell the pastor the vote of the committee. The pastor may then feel betrayed and wonder why he or she wasn't told directly. It is true that some danger is also involved in telling the pastor directly, since possibly no move can be arranged and the pastor may have to stay another year in the face of an adverse committee vote. But all things considered, the *Discipline* has wisdom on its side when it places the duty on the committee members to inform the pastor of their decision. The openness and honesty of this procedure make it the fairest possible way. In the matter of the new appointment of a pastor, the committee then works in an advisory way with the district superintendent and bishop. The ultimate appointment is with the bishop in consultation with the superintendents.

This committee also serves as personnel committee for all employed personnel, recommending personnel to the Administrative Board after consultation with the pastor. In churches with multiple staffs, the committee may be referred to as the Staff-Parish Relations Committee. Another important function of the committee is to interview persons of the local church seeking to be candidates for the ministry, and to make recommendations about them to the Charge Conference.

A third mandatory committee of great importance is the Committee on Finance. This is the group charged with budget making and budget raising. Like most other bodies of the church, it is amenable to the Administrative Board. This group needs to be a commonsense, hard-headed body, but it needs to avoid the temptation to let preconceived notions of "how much we can raise" determine and limit the church's program. That is, within reasonable limits, the Finance Committee ought to draw up budgets based upon projected programs; then it should spearhead the annual canvass with a maximum effort, letting the people decide through their pledges whether or not they will support the programs. If they will not, then is the time for the Finance Committee to trim back the budget to correspond to anticipated income. Then it can say, "I told you so," if it wants to, but not before then!

Summary

This, then, is the local church—the place "where the action is"—and because the action is always changing, the church's structure would be *semper reformanda*. United Methodism's flexible structure for the local church recognizes this truth.

Chapter IV

THE DIACONAL AND ORDAINED
MINISTRY

A ministerial friend of mine used to be fond of asserting that our church was "a benevolent theocracy." This remark is undoubtedly an exaggeration, but the fact remains that the clergy in United Methodism exercises a power far beyond what its numbers would indicate within the total structure. This fact can be understood only in the light of our historical background, in which our first and primary structures were the Annual Conferences of the preachers. This Annual Conference structure of "ministers only," so expedient and valid for a church following the frontier, continued to exist in Episcopal Methodism until 1939! In that year, with the reunion of Methodism, lay representation, with laypersons as actual members of the Annual Conference, was first adopted. The lay members of Annual Conference are becoming more effective with each passing year, but the ordained ministers, with their full-time involvement in the church and their lifetime membership in the Annual Conference, still do most of the talking and, generally, exert the greater leadership. This is not as true in the General Conference, where lay delegates are likely to have as much or more seniority than ministerial delegates; the ministerial delegates to the General Conference nevertheless are a very potent force. Couple these facts with the strong role the ordained minister occupies in the local church as pastor in charge and chairperson of the nominating committee, and the fact that district superintendents and bishops all come out of the ranks of the ordained ministry, and we begin to get some idea of the crucial part that the ordained ministry plays within the structure of United Methodism. It is for this reason that a chapter is devoted here to this subject and to the diaconal ministry.

The Diaconal Ministry

In chapter 2 of this book we described how the *Discipline* lays the groundwork for "The Ministry of All Christians," making it clear that all baptized Christians, lay and clergy, are called to this ministry. The theological rationale for this comes as chapter 1 of *The Book of Discipline*, fittingly preceding sections on the local church, on the diaconal ministry, and on the ordained clergy.

Chapter 2 of the *Discipline*, "The Diaconal Ministry," describes a particular office in the church, and describes the relationship of this office to the general ministry of all Christians in Par. 301:

The New Testament witness to Jesus Christ makes clear that the primary form of his ministry, in God's name, was that of service (diakonia) in the world. Very early in its history the Church came to understand that all of its members were commissioned, in baptism, to ministries of love, justice, and service, within local congregations and the larger communities in which they lived; all who follow Jesus have a share in the ministry of Jesus, who came not to be served, but to serve. There is thus a general ministry of all baptized Christians (Pars. 105-107).

The Church also affirms that particular persons are called and set apart for representative ministries of leadership within the body, to help the whole of the membership of the Church be engaged in and fulfill its ministry of service (Par. 109). The purpose of such leadership is the equipping of the general ministry of the Church, to the end that the whole Church may be built up as the Body of Christ for the work of ministry. This set-apart ministry is not a substitute for the diaconal responsibility of all members of the general ministry. Rather, it exists to intensify and make more effective the self-understanding of the whole People of God as servants in Christ's name.

The emphasis here is on a lay office, engaged in a serving ministry in a professional capacity for the church. Also emphasized is God's call to this ministry and the need of the church to authenticate this call.

Diaconal ministers must be recommended to the Annual Conference by the conference Board of Diaconal Ministry, for consecration by the bishop. When so consecrated, they become full voting members of the Annual Conference as part of the lay membership.

Diaconal ministers differ from the general ministry by reason of their professional serving ministry for the church. They differ from ordained ministers by reason of their lay status, their freedom from vows to accept a bishop's appointment (while appointed by a bishop, diaconal ministers or employing agencies take the initiative in employment, and the bishop's appointment, while a necessary and final step in the process, is not really determinative of the place of employment), and their serving functions in ways different from ministries of "Word, Sacrament, and Order."

The whole concept of diaconal ministry is still emerging and should become clearer as study continues concerning its role in the life of the church.

To sum up, diaconal ministry is one important facet of the general ministry of all Christians, which is defined in one other place in the *Discipline,* Par. 401:

Ministry in the Christian church is derived from the ministry of Christ, the ministry of the Father through the Incarnate Son by the Holy Spirit. It is a ministry bestowed upon and required of the entire Church. All Christians are called to ministry, and theirs is a ministry of the people of God within the community of faith and in the world. Members of The United Methodist Church receive this gift of ministry in company with all Christians and sincerely hope to continue and extend it in the world for which Christ lived, died, and lives again. The United Methodist Church believes that Baptism, confirmation, and responsible membership in the Church are visible signs of acceptance of this ministry.

This concise statement makes a number of things clear about what we mean by ministry. It is based on the ministry of Christ himself, who was not an ordained clergyman, but a layman. So if we want to know what it means to be a minister, we should look to Christ and see what he did. Ministry finds its perfect expression in him. The statement also makes it clear that the very fact of being a Christian carries with it the call to ministry. Furthermore, the ministry is twofold: it is within the community of faith and it is in the world. That is, Christians are called on to love and serve their brothers and sisters who are members of the church, but they are also called on to love and serve their brothers and sisters who are not. Thus, ministry recognizes no exclusive barriers.

The disciplinary statement also recognizes that ministry is a gift; a gift shared with all Christians. The last sentence affirms that when we are baptized, confirmed, and take up responsible membership in the church, we thereby visibly accept this ministry. So it is clear that the layperson in the pew is called to share in this ministry; the diaconal minister (Pars. 301-317) who serves the church in a professional capacity is also involved in ministry, though he or she is not ordained; and the ordained minister also shares in this general ministry, in addition to special responsibilities of ministry that will be discussed in the following section.

The Ordained Minister

Within the ranks of Christians who share in ministry, there are persons who are "called of God and set apart by the Church for the specialized ministry of Word, Sacrament, and Order" (Par. 402). These are the persons we commonly call "ministers," and the special task to which they are called we usually call "the ministry." Until 1976 the *Discipline* followed common usage and used the term "the ministry" to refer to the ordained ministry. But the growth of the concept of ministry in its various expressions convinced the General Conference of 1976 to clarify the disciplinary language and designate clergy as being "the ordained ministry."

Exactly what *is* the ministry to which certain persons in the church are "ordained," or for which they are set apart? It is described as a "ministry of Word, Sacrament, and Order." What is the "ministry of Word"? This is a ministry concerned with teaching and preaching the Word of God. So preaching and teaching stand

75

as primary functions of the ordained minister. The subject of this preaching and teaching is to be "the Word of God." While the term "Word of God" is often popularly identified with the Bible, we should note that the two terms are not synonymous. For instance, a preacher who picks some obscure passage out of the Bible and uses it as a text to preach a message of hatred may be preaching the Bible but is not preaching "the Word." On the other hand, it is difficult to imagine a preacher who is preaching the Word without also preaching the Bible, or being thoroughly grounded in it, for the Bible is our primary sourcebook for knowing what God's Word and will are for our lives. So the ministry of Word is a preaching and teaching ministry.

The ministry of Sacrament, as its name implies, involves the authorization to administer the sacraments of Baptism and the Lord's Supper. This function is one which clearly casts the ordained person in the role of priest, the keeper of "the holy of holies."

Finally, to be ordained to the ministry of Order is to be authorized to "equip the laity for ministry, exercise pastoral oversight, and administer the Discipline of the Church." Note the reemphasis here on the concept of ministry; one of the ordained minister's primary tasks is to prepare and equip the lay Christian to engage in ministry. The ministry of Order also includes exercising "pastoral oversight"; ordained ministers must not become so involved with equipping the laity for ministry that they forget to minister to the people under their care.

The ministry of Order lays upon the ordained person the necessity to "administer the Discipline of the Church." Sometimes ordained persons resent this last requirement, as it seems to put them in the place of representing the heavy hand of the institution. But most ministers, when they count up the high privileges that have been afforded to them by the institution, are happy and proud to administer its discipline; they recognize that it is not something handed down by the hierarchy, but something which has been hammered out by delegates to the General Conference elected by them, and represents the best thinking of hundreds of dedicated laypersons and ministers of the church. This last requirement of the ministry of Order, then, makes two things clear; that ordination is not only to the high and holy and priestly tasks, but also to the mundane, and that no person should seek ordination who is not willing in some sense to be an "institutional person." This is intended to mean only that he or she have some measure of belief and trust and confidence in the ordaining authority.

We may be puzzled when we seek to find the rationale for ordination. For the functions of the ordained minister that seem to require the least special training are those which are most jealously guarded. For instance, it is clear that the function of preaching and teaching the Word is one requiring a good deal of special training if it is to be done well; yet ministers are not at all reluctant about allowing laity to preach on occasion, and to do teaching. It is equally clear that the ministry of Order requires some training in the task of administration of the church; yet ministers welcome laity in administrative tasks, and many would be glad to turn over the whole administrative task to a layperson if they could. But the function of administering the sacraments is one which would look to the outside observer "like a cinch." Baptizing people or serving them bread and wine at Communion doesn't seem too hard—to require any special skills or training. Yet this function of the ordained ministry is guarded more jealously than any other! Why? Certainly not because the ordained person has any special training or qualifications which enables him or her to do it better than anyone else. The answer, rather, is to be found in the whole mystique that surrounds the idea of the priesthood.

From time immemorial, priests have been regarded as holy persons, guardians of sacred mysteries. For centuries Roman Catholic doctrine has taught that in the Mass, presided over by a priest, the bread and wine were actually changed then and there into the body and blood of Christ. This seems to point to a need which people have in their religions for some special acts to be performed by the priest, the "man of God" or the "woman of God." The Protestant doctrine of the priesthood of all believers has not eliminated this need, and practically all Protestant denominations, in varying degrees, continue to set aside certain acts as "priestly." These acts are usually those associated with the ministry of

Sacrament. Certainly this is true in United Methodism, where the sacramental privileges and responsibilities of the minister are deeply ingrained.

If you want to start a good argument among a group of ministers, ask the question: "What happens when you baptize an infant?" The answers are likely to range all the way from the minister who sees it purely symbolically—the baptism is a symbol of the entrance of the child into the Christian community as it is represented by its minister—to the minister who sees the baptism as a means of grace in which God is present in a special way, and in which the minister is a special channel of that grace. And the discussion is likely to be laden with some emotion, for these questions go to the very heart of a person's identity as a minister.

It is this same question of identity that is at the heart of discussions over questions such as apostolic succession, or "high church" vs. "low church," which also tend to be laden with some emotion. Is the minister just another guy or gal who happens to be doing a particular job, or is he or she a person under special orders from God? With our heads we tend to agree with the former, but with our hearts we agree with the latter. Thus, the fact that in United Methodism the administration of the sacraments is reserved for the minister is more a conviction of the heart than of the head; this in no way detracts from the conviction, for the fact is that often our finest and most important convictions are the very ones that cold logic is least able to back up.

This is not to say that United Methodism's view of ordination as being primarily related to the administration of the sacraments is one based solely on emotion. The noted United Methodist theologian, Dr. Albert Outler, has said this on the subject:

The preachers whom Wesley "employed" as his "helpers" in the leadership of the Methodist societies were, with few exceptions, laymen—i.e., baptized/confirmed Christians—whom he commissioned to assist him in the preaching of the gospel, in the direction of Christian nurture, and in the stewardship of the temporal economy of the Methodist societies. He steadfastly refused to ordain them (cf. the "Korah Sermon"). His sufficient warrant for this was his conviction that the Methodist people had normal access to the sacraments, at the hands of the ordained clergy of the Church of England. This means that John Wesley understood *ordination* as directly and uniquely correlated with *the administration of the sacraments* rather than with preaching and nurture. Here he stood with the nearly unanimous teaching in the Christian community throughout its history—that the sacraments are uniquely representative acts of the *whole* body of Christ's people (as preaching is not) and, hence, their administrants must be duly and fully *representative* of the whole church. Thus, ordination is an act of the whole church by which a person is designated as an authorized representative of the whole church, especially for those acts in which the whole church is symbolically represented. [1]

Thus, there is sound theological and historical basis for the preeminence of the sacramental in the United Methodist view of ordination.

This ministry of Word, Sacrament, and Order is shared by two orders of the ministry: deacons and elders. Deacon is the first ordination, and ordinarily takes place at the same time a person is received into an Annual Conference as a probationary member or an associate member. A probationary member is likely to remain a deacon for three or four years while completing the educational and other requirements for full membership in the conference, at which time he or she will be ordained an elder. An associate member may remain a deacon throughout his or her ministry. In either case, the deacon is given authority by ordination to perform most ministerial functions, except the administration of the sacraments, in which deacons may only *assist* an elder. However, if a deacon is regularly appointed to a pastoral charge, then he or she automatically receives full sacramental rights *on the charge* to which appointed. In other words, the right to administer the sacraments is "local," limited to the parish where the deacon is serving as pastor in charge. Thus, for instance, a deacon serving a charge would have full sacramental rights within that pastoral charge, but if asked to conduct a Communion service or administer a baptism at the Annual Conference or some other place, he or she would have to decline.

[1] Unpublished notes, "Problems of Order and Ordination in The Methodist Church."

After at least two years as a deacon, and the completion of the requirements leading to full membership and election thereto, candidates are eligible to be ordained as elders. Upon such ordination, they are entitled to full ministerial rights, not limited in any way, so long as they remain full members in good standing and conduct themselves in accordance with the *Discipline.*

The actual acts of ordination to both orders are presided over by a bishop. A bishop has authority to ordain only those persons who have been duly processed by the Annual Conference Board of Ordained Ministry, and for whom orders have been voted by the full ministerial members of the Annual Conference. In the "laying on of hands" for ordination as deacon, the bishop alone performs this act; in the ordination to the order of elder, the bishop is joined by other elders in the laying on of hands. Ordinations are usually done at the session of the Annual Conference, in an impressive service which is long remembered by those being ordained.

Qualifications and Training for the Ministry

The three traditional professions have been law, medicine, and the ministry. These professions have always required a high level of personal qualifications, physical stamina, and extensive academic preparation. The United Methodist ministry is no exception to this general rule, and a high school graduate wishing to enter our ministry must look forward to at least nine years of preparation before becoming a fully ordained minister: four years of college, three years of seminary, and two years on the field serving under the supervision of a district superintendent. So the process of preparation is a long and arduous one. This section will describe the process and the various levels in it.

Some explanation should be given at this point concerning the way in which the various levels of relationship to the Annual Conference are related to ordination. Perhaps the best way to describe this is that the person pursuing the ministry is moving up two ladders at the same time. One is the ladder of ordination, and the minister moving up its steps is establishing certain status and taking on certain responsibilities within the Church of God; the ordination ritual is couched entirely in this language, and does not even mention The United Methodist Church. The other is the ladder of Annual Conference relationship, and its various steps establish relationships specifically within The United Methodist Church. So when a minister has completed climbing both ladders he or she is a minister of the Church of God (by ordination) and a minister of The United Methodist Church (by virtue of Annual Conference relationship). It would be an oversimplification, however, to think of these two ladders as existing independently of each other, for they are tied together at many points, with progress on one being dependent upon progress on the other. Furthermore, the two-ladder theory does not give ministers the right to think that because they have been ordained as ministers in the Church of God, they are therefore responsible only to that church in the exercise of their ordination rights. The fact is that The United Methodist Church, which acts as an agent for the Church of God in the act or ordination, must continue to act as its agent in seeing to it that ordination rights are properly exercised. So the two ladders are interrelated in many ways, but they are still two ladders, and an understanding of this is essential to an understanding of the relationship between ordination and Annual Conference membership.

Every person who seeks to be a minister of our church must begin by qualifying as a candidate for ordained ministry. To do this, he or she must be a high school graduate who has been a member or an affiliate member of the local recommending congregation of The United Methodist Church for at least one year. He or she must receive the recommendation of the Charge Conference by a written two-thirds ballot after consultation and recommendation by the Pastor-Parish Relations Committee; this important first step must be taken with the utmost seriousness by the Charge Conference, since it is launching a person on a long and difficult journey toward a task that carries the gravest responsibilities. This grass-roots provision is intended to ensure that the people who know the candidate best are prepared to recommend him or her. The candidate must then after completing certain studies appear before the district Committee on Ordained

Ministry to be examined carefully concerning aptitudes and abilities, faith and commitment.

Furthermore, the candidate is required to agree to make a complete dedication to the highest ideals of the Christian life, and to this end agree to exercise responsible self-control by "personal habits conducive to bodily health, mental and emotional maturity, fidelity in marriage and celibacy in singleness, social responsibility, and growth in grace and the knowledge and love of God." This section was adopted at the Uniting 1968 Conference only after an explanatory note was also adopted for inclusion in the *Discipline* which makes it clear that this section in no way lessens the traditional concern of the church over the use of alcohol and tobacco by its ministers. The former Evangelical United Brethren Church had a provision (Par. 295, 1963 E.U.B. *Discipline*) which forbade licensing anyone to preach "who used tobacco or alcoholic beverages in any form"; the former Methodist Church had a provision (Par. 306.6, 1964 *Discipline*) which required the applicant for license to preach to agree to abstain "from all indulgences, including alcoholic beverages and tobacco, which may injure his influence." The new provision is simply an effort to remove the legalism while retaining the deep and valid concerns for the kind of witness a minister bears by personal habits and conduct. The 1984 General Conference added the words "fidelity in marriage and celibacy in singleness" in order to make clear long-standing moral expectations of clergy.

After satisfying the district Committee on Ordained Ministry on all these various counts, the candidate may then be granted certification as a candidate for ordained ministry. In order to continue as a candidate for ordained ministry, the person must pursue educational requirements from year to year in college, seminary, or with the Division of Ordained Ministry, all under the direction of the district Committee on Ordained Ministry, until such candidate qualifies as an associate or probationary member of an Annual Conference. At that time care for such persons shifts to the Annual Conference Board of Ordained Ministry.

Any candidate who wishes to serve as a pastor of a church must also qualify under Paragraph 406 for a license as a local pastor. This license confers the authority to preach and conduct worship in a church to which he or she may be appointed, and to administer the sacraments only for the duration of such appointment, and subject to annual renewal by the district Committee on Ordained Ministry. The holding of a license as local pastor does not make a person a minister; he or she is still a layperson who may be appointed only on a temporary basis (less than a year) to be a pastor. In order to retain this license, the licensee must satisfy the district Committee on Ordained Ministry each year that satisfactory progress is being made either in seminary studies or in the course of study administered by the Division of Ordained Ministry. So the holding of a license as a local pastor is not to be seen as an end in itself, but rather as a stepping stone on the way to the status of permanent local pastor or the ordained ministry.

LOCAL PASTORS. Because there is a persistent shortage of ministers to serve all the pastoral charges, the *Discipline* provides for a way in which a layperson may be appointed to serve as pastor of a charge. A layperson may do this by qualifying as a local pastor; this involves securing a license and being recommended annually by a vote of the district Committee on Ordained Ministry, the Board of Ordained Ministry, and finally, being approved as a local pastor by the full ministerial members of the Annual Conference. This approval does not guarantee an appointment; it only makes the person eligible to be appointed to be a pastor of a charge. Local pastors are placed in three categories by the Board of Ordained Ministry: full-time, part-time, and student. Persons in each category are required to make regular progress in their studies in order to remain local pastors.

A local pastor may perform all ministerial functions within the pastoral charge to which he or she is appointed (the laws of the state permitting), including administration of the sacraments for the duration of the appointment, subject to annual review. It should be pointed out, however, that some other persons listed as local pastors do have permanent authority to administer the sacraments, but this is because they have been ordained under rules and regulations of the former Evangelical United Brethren Church or the former Methodist Church, and these rights were specifically protected for them in the formation of The United Methodist Church. Nevertheless, these persons are listed with the local pastors, who are laypersons.

The 1980 General Conference took an action regarding full-time local pastors under appointment, classifying them as ministerial members of the Annual Conference (Par. 412.1). This action, undoubtedly taken in order to provide fairness for many full-time local pastors who serve the church very ably, has nevertheless introduced some extreme ambiguity into our understanding of ordination and of Annual Conference ministerial membership. Local pastors are not ordained and have always been considered laity; in fact, Paragraph 408.1 still defines them in this manner. Can a layperson also be a ministerial member of a conference? Paragraph 436 gives a guarantee of appointment to all ministerial members of the conference, which in Paragraph 412.1 clearly includes local pastors serving full-time. Does the General Conference really intend to grant such tenure? I believe not, but in rejecting proposed legislative clarifications, the 1984 General Conference did little to help this confusing situation.

ASSOCIATE MEMBERSHIP. Prior to the action of the 1980 General Conference that made local pastors who serve full-time ministerial members, it was clear that the associate member represented the crossing of the dividing line from laity to clergy, for the associate member is clearly a clergy person and ordained a deacon. (The person may have been ordained an elder under previous rules of the former churches, in which case that order is retained.) Associate membership is intended for persons who, for some good reason, are not in a position to secure the complete seminary education that is required for full membership, yet they wish to give their lives to the ministry and meet certain lesser educational requirements. A person seeking associate membership must qualify in these ways: he or she must be at least thirty-five years of age; must have served at least four years as a full-time local pastor and have completed the five-year course of study; must have completed a minimum of sixty semester hours of credit in college or have demonstrated an equivalent competency; must have been recommended by the district Committee on Ordained Ministry and the Board of Ordained Ministry, declared willingness to accept full-time appointment, satisfied the Board of his or her good health, submitted a sermon, and given satisfactory answers to doctrinal and other questions by the Board of Ordained Ministry.

An associate member who wishes to go on to full membership may do so, but only by going through probationary membership first. Associate members can vote in the Annual Conference on all matters except constitutional amendments, election of delegates to the General and Jurisdictional Conferences, and matters of ordination, character, and conference relations of ministers. They can serve on any board or commission or committee of the Annual Conference except the Board of Ordained Ministry. They are not eligible for election to General or Jurisdictional Conferences.

Associate membership provides a secure place within the ministry of our church for persons who often possess great gifts and are thoroughly dedicated to the ministry, but for whom circumstances prevent their securing the formal education required for full membership.

PROBATIONARY MEMBERSHIP. Probationary membership is in many ways similar to associate membership. Both carry with them ordination as deacon. Both involve the same voting rights in the Annual Conference. But the educational requirements differ, and a principal difference lies in the temporary nature of probationary membership as over against the usually permanent nature of associate membership.

Probationary membership, as its name implies, is a time "on trial"—a time of testing before final commitments to full membership are made. The basic educational requirement for admission to probationary status is the completion of at least one-half of the three-year seminary course.

In addition, the candidate must have been enrolled as a candidate for ordained ministry for at least one year, and be examined for the first time about the attitude of those close to him or her (such as a spouse) toward the ministry, for perhaps in no other field of work is this quite so important. The candidate is asked about debts, in an effort to make sure he or she will not be plagued by financial troubles in the ministry. Candidates are asked to reiterate their complete dedication to the Christian life and sound personal habits which were first agreed to when they became candidates for the ordained ministry. They are questioned about willingness to deal with all people in ministry without regard to race or national origin. In addition, they are required to present a written theological statement covering their basic beliefs and a written sermon on a specified biblical passage. In short, the candidate for probationary membership is rigorously examined by the district Committee on Ordained Ministry and by the Board of Ordained Ministry. Lest anyone think, however, that all of this sounds like too harrowing an experience, let it be emphasized that these groups of ministers are almost invariably warm and friendly, doing everything in their power to make the candidate feel at ease. Hopefully, they remember how they felt when they stood in the candidate's shoes!

The *Discipline* (Par. 416) does provide for an alternate procedure for attaining probationary membership "under special conditions." This may be used by an Annual Conference in two instances: for the candidate who has completed one-half of the seminary work in an accredited seminary but has done the undergraduate work in an unaccredited college; and for a person of thirty-five or more who has been an associate member for two years, is a college graduate, and has taken two years of advanced study under the Division of Ordained Ministry, and has been recommended by a three-fourths vote of the cabinet and the Board of Ordained Ministry for exhibiting "exceptional promise for the ministry." Many Annual Conferences follow a policy of not allowing for such exceptional cases. The *Discipline*, in fact, allows Annual Conferences to adopt rules which set the Master of Divinity degree as the minimum requirement for probationary membership.

Probationary members may continue in this relationship for a number of years, providing they are making regular progress in their theological studies. But the *Discipline* puts an absolute limit of eight years on the length of time a minister may remain a probationary member. In other words, if the person is not advanced to full membership within eight years, he or she must be discontinued. Discontinuance is the usual means by which a probationary member terminates or is terminated from this ministerial relationship, and such action has no reflection on his or her character.

FULL MEMBERSHIP. To be a member in full connection is the normative status for the United Methodist minister, and the great majority of local churches are served by pastors who hold this relationship. Election to full membership qualifies the minister to be ordained an elder, the higher order in the church. Full membership brings with it full voting rights in the Annual Conference, and sole responsibility along with the other members in full connection for all matters of ordination, character, and conference relations of ministers. For the first time he or she becomes eligible to be elected a delegate to General or Jurisdictional Conference. In other words, the minister-in-the-making has at last become a full-fledged minister!

In order to arrive at this point, the minister was a probationary member at least two years, graduated with a Master of Divinity degree or its equivalent from a properly accredited seminary, was previously ordained a deacon, and served full time under episcopal appointment under the supervision of a district superintendent for two years following seminary graduation. Some Annual Conferences may provide for a longer period of service under a superintendent. Again, there is an alternate route provided, by which the candidate who was accepted as a probationary member under exceptional circumstances (Par. 416) may satisfy the seminary graduation requirement with two more years of advanced study with the Division of Ordained Ministry (Par. 424). However, it should again be stressed that this provision is not operative in many Annual Conferences which have adopted a "seminary rule" requiring the basic seminary degree for any candidate for full membership; and even where a conference has no such rule, the provision of a nonseminary route to full membership is clearly intended to be for the genuinely exceptional case, and thus should rarely be invoked.

The candidate for full membership is further required to satisfy the board as to his or her physical, mental, and emotional health. It should be mentioned that most Boards of Ordained Ministry regularly employ psychological testing at this point and earlier points in the candidate's progress. Such testing is often an extremely useful aid in helping the board make its decisions concerning the candidates; but it should be just that—an aid—and not the determinative factor. Psychologists can be wrong, too!

The candidate must also submit a written sermon on a specified biblical text and take a written doctrinal examination. In this connection, it is safe to say that most Boards or Ordained Ministry are not so much interested in the various shades of theological opinion reflected in the answers as they are in seeing how well the candidate wrestles with the question and grasps essentials of the issues.

The final step into full membership occurs when the candidates appear before the Annual Conference and are asked by the bishop a series of questions first asked by John Wesley. The language of the questions is somewhat quaint, but the meaning of most is unmistakable. One suspects that embarrassment over these questions is not due so much to their quaint language and form as it is to their blunt and brutal directness (e.g., "Are you in debt so as to embarrass you in your work?").

When a minister is finally voted into full connection by the other ministers in full connection, it is a high moment, the culmination of years of education and preparation. But lest any ministers feel that being voted full connection means they have "arrived," let them take a careful look at the provisions of our *Discipline* concerning continuing education (Par. 445). This healthy and needed emphasis in our church is intended to ensure that the minister's education will go on throughout his or her career. The whole church needs to be increasingly aware of this relatively new emphasis in our ideas of how a minister should be educated.

Relationship to the Annual Conference:
A Distinctive Feature of the United Methodist Ministry

It would be inaccurate to say that the United Methodist minister's relationship to the Annual Conference is something absolutely unique to our clergy. Certainly some of the Roman Catholic orders possess much the same spirit of community and of being under orders that we do. A Presbyterian minister bears certain relationships to the presbytery that are in many ways similar to our relationships to our Annual Conference. Nevertheless, it can be safely said that among Protestant denominations as a whole, the kind of relationship that a United Methodist minister bears to the Annual Conference is a distinctive one. The *Discipline* offers this brief description:

Members in full connection with an Annual Conference by virtue of their election and ordination are bound in special covenant with all the ordained ministers of the Annual Conference. In the keeping of this covenant they perform the ministerial duties and maintain the ministerial standards established by those in the covenant. They offer themselves without reserve to be appointed and to serve, after consultation, as the appointive authority may determine. They live with their fellow ordained ministers in mutual trust and concern and seek with them the sanctification of the fellowship (Par. 422).

This "special covenant" is most vividly reinforced each year when the ministers meet in executive session at Annual Conference (a closed session of members in full connection only) to consider matters of "ordination, character, and conference relations of ordained ministers." In other words, it is a time of the making and unmaking of ministers. Sometimes a candidate for membership will be the son or daughter of one of the members, and the parent may make the motion to grant membership and say a few words on behalf of this special person; sometimes members who have been pastors of a candidate as he or she grew up and made the decision for the ministry will speak on this person's behalf; these are times when the covenant takes on a special joy. Regrettably, in large conferences where scores of ordinands are being voted upon, time for such expressions seems to get squeezed out.

There are other times when painful separation takes place, as when ministers leave the fellowship. These ministers may feel they have not been fairly dealt with by their superiors, and as members of the fellowship until they are actually voted out by the group, they may speak their minds to their brothers and sisters. Sometimes if there is suspicion that the person who is leaving has been unfairly forced out by the bishop and cabinet, members may direct pointed questions to the district superintendents and to the bishop, and they had better be prepared to answer them with candor. Such questioning is perfectly proper, because the final responsibility for each person's ministerial status rests solely with one's ministerial colleagues of the conference. Almost always there is an openness and concern evident in these sessions which, even in situations of great pain and distress, result in a strengthening of the covenant and a renewed joy in being part of such a fellowship.

Part of the strength of the covenant results from the commonly shared willingness to go where appointed. The appointive system as such will be discussed later, but there is no question that the sharing of this kind of willingness to accept one's appointment helps create the unity that comes from a shared discipline.

An important part of the secret of the power of this covenant lies in the fact that, in a very real sense, the Annual Conference is the only home that ministers of our church have. This statement will probably be disputed by some ministers, but in the early days of our church it was quite literally true. The circuit rider had no home; he constantly traveled his circuit, and the one point of reference he had each year was his Annual Conference. This was home for him. He was called a "traveling preacher," and this term is still used today synonymously with a ministerial member of an Annual Conference. It is true, of course, that ministers today have become much more settled—living in parsonages, raising families, staying in one community a number of years. But United Methodist ministers are not as likely to think of the places they are living as home as are persons in other occupations who may move just as often or oftener. Part of this may be due to the parsonage system, but part is surely due to the covenant relationship with brothers and sisters in the Annual Conference.

An interesting aspect of this has to do with the question of where the minister's church membership is located. This is a question which reveals a sharp difference of opinion between ministers of the former Methodist Church and ministers of the former Evangelical United Brethren Church. In The Methodist Church, by long-standing tradition rather than specific disciplinary provision, ministers were not considered members of a local church. Rather, their church membership was in the Annual Conference, in line with their status as traveling preachers. So when a typical Methodist minister was given a new appointment, he would arrange for the transfer of his wife's and family's membership to the church of which he was now pastor, but not his own, because his membership stayed with the Annual Conference. In The Evangelical United Brethren Church, by contrast, the *Discipline* specifically stated that "every minister shall maintain membership in some local church." Furthermore, the local church membership of the minister and family was considered automatically transferred to a new pastoral assignment (Par. 255, 1963 E.U.B. *Discipline*). The minister was also a member of the Annual Conference, of course, so maintained a dual relationship.

What is the situation in United Methodism? The issue was deliberately not resolved at the Uniting Conference, because the Committee to Study the Ministry found this was one of the few issues they were unable to resolve during their four-year study prior to the Uniting Conference. So presumably ministers of both former churches are continuing their customary practices, and our statisticians are working to find ways to be sure they are neither counting ministers twice nor not counting them at all! But aside from any statistical problems this unresolved issue may be causing, there are serious differences of basic ecclesiology.

What is the church, and what does it mean to be a member of it? The E.U.B. view stressed the importance of being a part of a local congregation, and seems to say that a person cannot be a member of the church without also being a member of a local church—that there is something unreal about church membership which is not tied into a local fellowship of worshiping and working persons. The Methodist Articles of Religion would seem to give some backing to this position in the definition of the church as "a congregation of faithful men." At any rate, membership in a local congregation is a very meaningful thing for many former E.U.B. ministers, and they cherish this while still lifting up the importance of their relationship to the Annual Conference. The traditional Methodist view, on the other hand, is based on an ecclesiology not so tied to the local congregation, and admits the possibility of membership in the church at levels other than the local. Methodist fears in regard to a minister's holding membership in his or her local church seem to center in the area of amenability. To whom is the minister answerable! Strict logic would seem to indicate that if the minister is a member of the congregation, he or she would be amenable to them. However, actual E.U.B. practice, as indicated in their *Discipline*, shows that amenability of ministers to the Annual Conference is clearly set forth, and there is no practical difference in amenability from the Methodist position. Another fear expressed is that it would be embarrassing for district superintendents and bishops to have to decide which local church they will join. But the former E.U.B. bishops and superintendents have been doing this for years with no apparent ill effects, and spouses and families of these officers have to choose a church to join under Methodist practice. The fact is that this issue, seen from the standpoint of the average layperson in the pew, is a tempest in a teapot. It would seem that a way could be found to preserve the United Methodist ministers' distinctive relationship to their Annual Conferences and at the same time make it possible for them to be members of the local congregation. United Methodist legislative ingenuity will surely find an answer to the present impasse which will not diminish the "special covenant" each minister has with ministerial colleagues of the conference. However, the foregoing lines, written in 1969, have not proved true as of 1988.

The Pastor's Job Description

Every pastor of every United Methodist church, large or small, has a job description spelled out in our *Discipline* (Pars. 439-441).

92

I will not attempt to spell out the points here, but only comment on some of the requirements.

Under their general responsibility to supervise the work and program of the local church, pastors are required to give account of their ministry to the Charge and Annual Conferences," according to the prescribed forms." This is one of those mundane responsibilities of institutional pencil-pushing which pastors sometimes resent. But this reporting is simply a matter of communication on what is happening, and the amount of statistical reporting required of a United Methodist minister is minimal compared to the reporting requirements of 90 percent of the jobs that laypersons hold. Ministers should be glad to do the reporting which is required of them. This same paragraph makes clear the pastor's responsibility to participate in denominational and conference programs and training opportunities; this, too, is part of the job of a pastor.

One of the pastoral duties is to perform the marriage ceremony, but the decision to perform it or not in any given case is the pastor's to make. He or she is admonished to provide due counsel to the parties, and is given guidance on the matter of the marriage of divorced persons. He or she is called upon to counsel persons under threat of marriage breakdown, and bereaved persons, and to call in the homes of the parish and community.

Pastors have a specific responsibility to instruct candidates for church membership and to receive them into the church. They are also charged with the task of seeking out persons who may make decisions for Christian service and counsel them in this regard. Another responsibility is "to participate in the life and work of the community and in ecumenical concerns and to lead the congregation to become so involved" (Par. 439.1*l*). This, of course, points to the need to give of themselves beyond the walls of their own local churches.

This paragraph, then, constitutes the United Methodist minister's job description. In recent years, some pastors and congregations have been involved in so-called "contracting," as though a pastor's job description was something to be negotiated between a pastor and an individual congregation. This is not the case in United Methodism. Pastors and congregations should have good understandings with one another, but always within the context of the job description provided in Paragraphs 439-441.

The pastor has one of the most exciting jobs there is on the face of the earth; the variety and challenge of the job are always more than a match for anyone's powers and energies. But it is a job that carries with it some of the highest vocational satisfactions that a person can know.

Other Tasks of Ministers

Ministers are involved in a number of tasks other than serving as pastors of local churches. Some six hundred in the United States are district superintendents, and forty-nine are active bishops. But in addition to these persons in the direct line of ecclesiastical authority there are several thousand in what the *Discipline* refers to as appointments beyond the local church. These ministers are working in a wide variety of tasks to which they are appointed by the bishop as outlined in Paragraph 443. These tasks fall into several categories.

The first is when a minister is appointed "within the connectional structures of United Methodism." This category includes district superintendents, Conference Council on Ministries staff, and others who are clearly within our denominational structures. But it also includes ministers appointed as "staff members of ecumenical agencies." Just how a staff member of Heifer Project, for instance, can be considered to be within "the connectional structures of United Methodism" is a little hard to figure out.

The second category is the appointment of persons "under endorsement by the Division of Chaplains and Related Ministries." This includes military, institutional, and other chaplains.

A third category is "appointments beyond the ministries usually extended through the local church and institutions referred to in the first two categories." Appointments in this group require approval by the bishop, cabinet, Board of Ordained Ministry, and a two-thirds vote of the ministerial members of the Annual

Conference. This category of appointments tends to become the farthest removed from the appointive power of the bishop and the effective discipline of the Annual Conference. The authority here is so broad and vague that almost any kind of work may be involved, and it is not hard to show that "ministry" is a part of almost any occupation. Should a minister be appointed as a grade-school teacher, or a counselor with a Dale-Carnegie-type private enterprise, or as a state employee working with alcoholics, or a family court commissioner, or any of scores of other positions that undoubtedly involve ministry? Recent General Conferences have wrestled with this matter and some progress is being made. A provision adopted in 1980 requires the bishop to meet at least annually with all persons in such appointments. This is leading to better understanding, but it will continue to be a knotty problem.

A fourth category of these appointments is school attendance. Although there is no salary involved here, under certain conditions there may be pension responsibilities carried by the Annual Conference. In these cases the ministers may be in school far away from the conference, perhaps pursuing graduate degrees, and amenability to the appointive power of the bishop tends to be diminished. For instance, these ministers may have finished two years of study and the bishop would like them to come home and take appointments as pastors. However, if they write back that they plan to continue their education another year, and that perhaps have received a grant for some special research, most bishops will be reluctant to order them home. But eventually the minister must make a decision to resume his or her regular vocation.

These, then, are the categories of "appointments beyond the local church" as spelled out in Paragraph 443.1. While it is clear that all such persons remain under the appointive authority of the bishop *de jure*, they tend to become less subject to it *de facto* as the years go by. So while theoretically the bishop has the power to appoint a university president who is a member of the conference to be the pastor of any church under the bishop's jurisdiction, it happens infrequently. If the bishop tried to force the issue against the desire of the minister and the university's board of trustees, the minister could always withdraw from the conference and as a layperson continue as university president, assuming the university were agreeable.

One of the potential dangers in broadening the field of appointments beyond the local church is in so diluting the concept of what it means to be an ordained minister that the ministry of "Word, Sacrament, and Order" loses its significance. The potential practical threat exists that large numbers of ministers in these special appointments could be determining the program of the Annual Conference which the pastors and lay members of the conference would then have to finance and carry out. This is probably somewhat remote, but it illustrates the need for some very serious thinking and legislation which will more adequately spell out the entire rationale and philosophy of such appointments. The 1976 and 1980 General Conference legislation is a step in the right direction.

After this discussion of some of the problems connected with special appointments, it needs to be added that this process is a source of great strength for our church. All the chaplains in military service and institutions are in their tasks under special appointment, and they are fulfilling a great need. It is impossible to assess the tremendous influence which our clergy have had as faculty members and administrators of our church-related colleges and universities. The special appointment has been one of the ways the church has ministered to the world and not simply to the people within the walls of the church building. And when ministers in these appointments take their disciplinary responsibilities seriously (Par. 443), they can be of tremendous help to the conference and to their district superintendent in the regular work of the church.

Another task of ministers is to serve as a "counseling elder" (Par. 411). Unlike the special appointment, this is not the full-time job of a minister, but a nonpaid task for which he or she is recommended by the Board of Ordained Ministry and to which he or she is assigned by the cabinet. The counseling elder's responsibility is to provide counsel for local pastors (usually located nearby) in fulfilling the requirements of their course of study, in developing their spiritual life, in the administration of the sacraments, and other aspects of the practice of ministry. This provision, adopted at the Uniting Conference, is a recognition that it is unfair both to the untrained local pastor and to the church involved for him or her to be left unaided with the responsibility of a pastorate. True, the district superintendent is able to provide some of this counsel, but not really enough. As the name implies, the counseling elder does not carry authority over the local pastor, but is a counselor, working under the direction of, and in consultation with, the district superintendent, making annual reports to him or her and to the Board of Ordained Ministry. The role of the counseling elder should be an increasingly important one in providing the most adequate ministry possible for all the congregations of United Methodism.

Other Ministerial Relationships and Termination Procedures

All the areas of the ministry which have been discussed to this point have been areas of active service. We now turn to some inactive ministerial relationships and to the ways in which termination of ministerial status may be effected.

SABBATICAL LEAVE. After a minister has served in full connection for six years, or as an associate member for eight years, he or she is entitled to ask for a year off for purposes of an approved program of study or travel (Par. 446). The person requesting such sabbatical leave should submit plans at least six months in advance to the Board of Ordained Ministry. Recommendations are then made to the Annual Conference for its action and appointment to sabbatical leave by the bishop. The intent of this provision is to give a minister a year away for purposes which should help to enrich his or her future ministry. It is not really intended for the minister who wants to leave the ministry, or for the one who wants a year of grace to try out a new job. However, requests for sabbaticals are often made on this basis, and in each case the Board of Ordained Ministry must evaluate it. If the minister is definitely leaving the ministry, then a sabbatical is not appropriate. But if there is some doubt or uncertainty on that question, Boards of Ordained Ministry usually tend to go along with the request, on the theory that this year away doing something else may well serve the purpose of a sabbatical in preparing the person to come back a year later with renewed zest for the job. The minister on sabbatical leave retains full standing in the conference, the conference share of his or her pension is paid during the year (subject to provisions of Par. 1606.3a), but no salary is received. The brutal fact about sabbaticals is that most ministers can never afford to take one, even though they are entitled to take one every seven years. It was probably in response to this situation that the 1976 General Conference made provision for "educational leaves" of up to six months, to be negotiated between the pastor, the district superintendent, and the Pastor-Parish Relations Committee, with the understanding that the pastor would come back to the same appointment (Par. 445.3). Some Annual Conferences have developed plans whereby funds are made available for such leaves. These funds make it possible for the pastor on leave to receive a stipend, and for the church to receive enough financial help to pay for a supply pastor during such absence. It seems clear that some such type of program will have to become widespread before the opportunity for leave for educational and renewal purposes will take on much meaning for the average minister.

DISABILITY LEAVE. A minister who has been forced to give up work because of physical or mental disability may be granted a disability leave by the full ministerial members of the Annual Conference, on joint recommendation of the conference Board of Pensions and the Board of Ordained Ministry. This involves certain medical examinations at the time the leave is granted, and each year as it is renewed by the conference. The Board of Pensions provides for a disability benefit for the minister during the period of disability leave. The disability leave terminates with either a return to active service or reaching the age of voluntary retirement.

MATERNITY/PATERNITY LEAVE. The 1976 General Conference, in response to growing numbers of women in the ranks of the clergy, adopted provisions for maternity leave, later changed to Maternity/Paternity Leave. These provide basically for up to three months' leave, with at least six weeks' salary guaranteed, with responsibility for continued pastoral service during such leaves in the hands of the district superintendent and the Pastor-Parish Relations Committee.

LEAVE OF ABSENCE. This is a category for ministers who "because of impaired health, emotional and/or physical exhaustion, ineffectiveness or incompetence, or other equally sufficient reason, are temporarily unwilling or unable to perform the duties of full-time itinerant ministry." This differs from disability leave in that the person is not completely disabled; for various reasons he or she feels temporarily unable to perform *full* work. This relationship permits continued standing as a member of the conference, although years on leave of absence are not counted as pension years. This relationship may be initiated either by the minister or by the cabinet. If the leave is initiated by the cabinet, the minister has a right to a hearing before the bishop, cabinet and executive committee of the Board of Ordained Ministry. He or she may not, however, continue in this relationship longer than five consecutive years, except on recommendation of the Board of Ordained Ministry and two-thirds vote of the conference.

RETIREMENT. The retired members of the Annual Conference are no longer under obligation to accept appointment from the bishop, but some continue to do so somewhat in the role of a supply pastor. They continue to be members of the Annual Conference and are entitled to vote therein throughout their lifetime. There are several ways in which retirement can take place:

1. Under Paragraph 451.3, "the Annual Conference . . . may place any ministerial members in the retired relation with or without their consent and irrespective of their age if such relation is recommended by the Board of Ordained Ministry and the Cabinet." This seems to be a sort of last-resort provision designed to care for the minister who isn't sick enough to be disabled, isn't old enough to be retired in the usual manner, isn't ineffective enough to be terminated by the conference, and for whom no proper appointment can be found. Solution: retirement, even at the age of twenty-nine years! Actually, this provision is probably infrequently

used. The 1984 General Conference added a provision giving a person so retired a right to a trial, if so requested.

2. Under Paragraph 451.1, if a minister reaches the age of seventy prior to July 1, he or she shall be automatically retired at the Annual Conference session for that year.

3. Under Paragraph 451.2c, if a minister has reached the age of sixty-five on or before July 1, or completed forty years of service prior to the opening day of the conference, he or she *may* be retired. In actual practice, a minister who qualifies for this permissive retirement and requests it is almost automatically granted it, but the language of the *Discipline* suggests that the conference is not under disciplinary compulsion to grant retirement. He or she *"may* be placed in the retired relation."

4. Paragraph 451.2a provides that a minister who has served for twenty years may also request retirement, with the privilege of receiving a pension when he or she reaches age sixty-two, based on years of service. This provision was first adopted at the Uniting Conference, and some concern has been expressed since that time about its effect. It is true that many private and governmental agencies may offer retirement after twenty years of service, but the person retired does not them retain a voice and vote in the organization. But in The United Methodist Church, a retired minister remains a voting member of the conference. Thus, the twenty-year retirement policy creates a group of retired ministers in the Annual Conference who cast votes on programs which the working pastors and laity will have to carry out and budgets which the working pastors and laity will have to raise. The expressed reason given for this new provision of the floor of the Uniting Conference was as follows: "The essence of it is that if any man has been in the conference for 20 years or more of full-time approved service and then goes into, say college teaching or something else, that would not be thereby appointed, he will not be deprived of using these 20 years when he comes to retirement as far as his annuity claim is concerned" (1968 *Daily Christian Advocate*, page 765). This legislation only gives the minister the right to *request* retirement after twenty years; the Board of Ordained Ministry and the conference are under no obligation to grant the request.

Another possibility of retirement is provided in Paragraph 453.2*b* for a minister who has served at least thirty-seven years or has reached age sixty-two by the June 30 closest to the Annual Conference session.

The retired minister still remains under the discipline of the conference, the district superintendent, and the pastor; he or she has a seat in the Charge Conference, and is required to report all marriages and baptisms to it. With the shortage of ministers in so many places, he or she is often asked to take a small appointment. He or she is free to decline but often agrees and makes possible a continuing ministry in places where otherwise there might be none.

TERMINATION OF THE MINISTRY. Sometimes ministers cease to be ministers, either of their own will or involuntarily. What are the ways this may take place within The United Methodist Church?

1. *Honorable Location.* This is one way in which a minister in good standing who desires to discontinue regular ministerial work may do so. The term "location" is an old one, referring to the fact that whereas he or she has been a traveling preacher, he or she now desires to become a local preacher. This involves giving up conference membership and standing, but not ordination rights, which he or she may continue to exercise under the supervision of the pastor in charge within the bounds of the charge. The minister still remains amenable to the Annual Conference for his or her conduct and the continuance of his or her ordination rights. If the person desires to be readmitted to the conference at some time, he or she is usually welcomed back. In some ways honorable location is not really termination of ministry, since the person retains ordination rights, although no longer a conference member.

2. *Involuntary Termination of Conference Membership.* This area received a great deal of attention at the 1980 General Conference, resulting in Paragraph 453. The 1984 General Conference further refined the procedures. A rather elaborate procedure is provided for handling grievances made about a minister. After ordinary supervisory and administrative measures have failed, there is a provision for a joint review committee, made

up of two superintendents appointed annually by the bishop, two Board of Ordained Ministry members nominated by the chairperson and elected annually by the Board, and two non-Cabinet, non-Board members in full connection, one nominated by the bishop and Cabinet, one by the Board, and elected annually by the members in full connection in ministerial Executive Session. The joint review committee, working informally and confidentially, seeks to resolve the matter, and makes its report and any recommendations to the Board of Ordained Ministry. The Board then may recommend any of a whole series of remedial actions, it may refer the matter to the Committee on Investigation for a possible trial, or it may recommend termination of membership. If it recommends the latter, the minister involved may either elect trial or withdraw under complaints as an alternative to being terminated. It can be seen that every protection is provided for the minister, but one wonders how much is provided for the church.

Paragraph 453.3, providing for administrative location, was submitted to the 1980 General Conference by the Council of Bishops as a way to deal with a long-standing problem, that of ministerial incompetence. It was debated at length, and adopted by a fairly narrow vote. Its intention was to provide an administrative way in which to deal with this problem, with adequate safeguards for the minister involved; but the legislation as adopted in 1980 and amended in 1984 made it clear that a minister who becomes the subject of administrative location procedures may choose a trial.

This rendered the procedure nearly unusable. But the 1988 General Conference amended this to delete the option of a trial, while providing for a full hearing. This should allow for use of this procedure in appropriate cases, while still safeguarding the rights of the clergy involved.

3. *Discontinuance from Probationary Membership.* This is a procedure applicable only to probationary members, whereby membership can be terminated at any time without reflection on the character of the minister involved. It simply recognizes that probationary membership is what it says it is—a time on trial, during which the member has no particular rights of "tenure." The

fact that such a person is required to surrender the deacon's credentials is no reflection upon him or her, but simply a recognition that a probationer's deacon's orders, unlike an associate member's, are transitory on the way to elder's orders.

4. *Withdrawal by Surrender of the Ministerial Office.* This is a voluntary action of a minister who simply desires no longer to be a minister; it goes further than honorable location, since it involves the voluntary surrender of credentials, the giving up of all ministerial and ordination rights and becoming a layperson.

5. *Withdrawal to Unite with Another Denomination.* This is also a voluntary action by a minister who desires to unite with another denomination. If so desired and approved by the conference, his or her credential may then be endorsed on the back, indicating voluntary and honorable dismissal, and returned to the minister.

6. *Withdrawal Under Charges.* A minister accused of certain offenses under the law of the church may be permitted to withdraw under charges and to surrender his or her credentials.

7. *Judicial Procedure.* Though very seldom used, this is a procedure which could result in a minister's being deposed from the ministry or expelled from the church after he has been tried and found guilty of one of the offenses listed in Paragraph 2621.

Summary

The ordained ministry of The United Methodist Church constitutes a community which is precious to its members. It is a fellowship based on shared hopes and dreams, tears and laughter, successes and failures. It is a coming together of a group of some of the most highly trained, socially aware, spiritually sensitive, and fiercely independent thinking souls on the face of the earth! What binds this highly variegated group together? One thing: they are under orders to be ministers of "Word, Sacrament, and Order," accepting their appointments "with a glad mind and will." To this high calling the ordained ministry of our church gives its life.

Chapter V

THE SUPERINTENDENCY

Until the 1976 General Conference, the duties of superintending, which in The United Methodist Church are in the hands of bishops and district superintendents, were included in the same chapter of the *Discipline* with all other matters of the ordained ministry. This had real validity, because in our structure all of these personnel are ordained, and the work they do is clearly a part of the work of ordained ministry. It was with some reluctance that in a prior edition I decided to follow the *Discipline's* lead and put superintendency in a separate chapter, since this carries some implication that the task is not a part of ordained ministry.

However, the change in Disciplinary arrangement grew out of an important study of superintendency carried on by a study commission in the 1972-76 quadrennium, in which the theological grounding of this task was clearly delineated for the first time.

The Nature of Superintendency

The *Discipline* (Pars. 501-502) makes clear that superintendency in The United Methodist Church resides in the office of bishop and extends to the district superintendent, with each possessing distinct responsibilities. Attention is called to the fact that such superintending has been a part of the church since apostolic times.

Paragraph 502 gives guidelines for superintending, under the themes of mode, pace, and skill. These spell out characteristics and qualities of leadership necessary to anyone who would serve either as a district superintendent or a bishop in The United Methodist Church.

Let us now look at each of these offices separately.

The District Superintendent

We have already seen in an earlier chapter that the district superintendent fills what is perhaps the most crucial role in connectional United Methodism. In many ways, he or she *is* the connector, the visible symbol to the laity of the local church of United Methodism as a whole. It is, then, of utmost importance that persons appointed as superintendents merit the trust and respect of both the ministers and laity of the conference. No more crucial decision is made by a bishop than that which is made in the appointment of superintendents, and the wise bishop is thinking years ahead on these matters.

The districts of United Methodism vary greatly in size, depending on population density and factors of geography. Some districts have as few as twenty churches, while others have over a hundred. But the basic tasks of every "D.S." are indicated in Paragraphs 519-524. In the pursuit of these duties the D.S. is likely to spend a proportionately larger share of time with the smaller churches than with the larger ones. The larger churches tend to have adequate leadership who can largely care for their problems, while the small and struggling congregations need more help. Thus, there is a real sense in which the district superintendent is also the "district missionary," helping provide the ministry of the church in locations where, but for this help, it could not survive.

One of the duties of a district superintendent is to be a pastor to pastors and their families. Everyone recognizes that because superintendents are authority figures, pastors often feel reluctant to counsel with them freely about their problems. Yet it is amazing how much counseling does take place, and the relationship between district superintendents and their pastors can be warm and meaningful. All things considered, if pastors had to choose between a superintendent who possessed some authority and one who was a counselor pure and simple, many would choose the authority, for to feel the backing of authority is one of the sources of strength for the pastor.

Exactly wherein does the district superintendent's authority lie? It is clear that he or she has no authority to tell a local pastor what to do. The pastor is the pastor *in charge*, and responsible for what happens in the church. The D.S. also has no authority to tell the laity what to do; they are governed in their actions by the policy of the Administrative Board and of their pastor.

The true authority of the district superintendent, then, is more indirect than direct, and is revealed in two areas. First, he or she is charged with seeing that the provisions of the *Discipline* are observed. This means that if a local church is planning to do something which is not in accord with the *Discipline* the superintendent has the duty and the responsibility to see that its provisions are abided by. This is also, of course, the duty of the pastor. The second and even more important source of authority of the superintendent is the fact that he or she carries an important role in the appointive process for ministers and churches. The laity and pastors know that the bishop relies heavily on the superintendent for counsel in appointments, and it is this fact which gives the superintendent significant authority.

Superintendents are limited to serving not more than six consecutive years in the office, and must be out of the office for at least three intervening years before being eligible to be appointed again. Furthermore, they cannot serve more than twelve years in their lifetime. There is a difference of opinion over this policy, with some feeling that a superintendent is just getting to know the job when it is time to leave it. Some also feel that the policy puts our superintendents at a disadvantage in ecumenical dealings with executives of other denominations, who often spend most of a lifetime in an executive position. On the other hand, majority sentiment still favors the six-year term as a way of curbing tendencies toward too much power, and also as a way of ensuring that superintendents will remain close to the problems of the pastorate. It is a way of saying that D.S.'s are basically pastors who are serving as superintendents for a while. And there is no question that there is an almost subconscious tempering of the way in which a superintendent treats a pastor growing from the knowledge that one day that pastor might be his or her superintendent. Whether all of this is evidence of strength or of weakness is surely debatable, but it would appear that a limitation on the term of superintendents will be with us for some time.

The issue of the appointive as against the elective superintendency was resolved at the Uniting Conference in favor of the appointive. However, the appointive principle was not made a constitutional matter, but a matter of legislation (Par. 517). Thus, this could be changed by the General Conference if they saw fit to do it. No attempt will be made here to set forth detailed argumemts on either side of this issue. Suffice it to say that on the side of the former E.U.B. practice of election is the whole thrust of democratic philosophy—that a group ought to be able to choose its own leaders and provide a democratic check on their exercise of leadership. On the side of the appointive superintendency is the point made by many modern students of government—that when you have provided for a democratic election of your chief officer, the interests of good government then dictate that he or she must have the authority to appoint the officers who are to serve that administration. As one who has served as both pastor and superintendent, I feel strongly that the appointive superintendency is essential to the effective functioning of leadership in our church—even more essential, in fact, than the life tenure of our bishops. The findings of the Study Commission on the Episcopacy and District Superintendency adopted by the 1976 General Conference add strength to the appointive principle in their conclusion that the district superintendency is an extension of the general superintendency.

The late Bishop G. Bromley Oxnam used to refer to the fact that the system of pastor-direct superintendent-bishop meant that every last corner of the United States, no matter how small or remote, was known by and covered by these persons; a record which few, if any, sales organizations could match! The district superintendent is a key person in this remarkable structure.

The Episcopacy

Bishops are considered by The United Methodist Church to be persons in whom the office of superintendency resides. This involves solemn and sacred responsibilities. Yet it should be clear that in our tradition bishops are not "ordained" as bishops; they are simply elected and consecrated to an "office." They function under the same ordination as every other elder in the church.

Bishops are elected by the Jurisdictional Conferences in the United States and by Central Conferences in other parts of the world. The conference then, on recommendation of its Committee on Episcopacy, assigns the bishop to a residence. The College on Bishops of the Jurisdictional or Central Conference assigns the bishops to residential and presidential supervision over one or more Annual Conferences, which assignment (and the geographical territory covered by it) is known as an "episcopal area." (See Judicial Council decision 517).

Bishops of The United Methodist Church, contrary to some popular opinion, do not possess unlimited power. The fact is that their powers are quite severely circumscribed by the Constitution and *Discipline* of the church. For instance, they do not possess a vote in the General Conference and cannot even speak on an issue there without the permission of the body. The same situation prevails in the Jurisdictional Conference. The bishop is the presiding officer of the Annual Conference, but as one who is not a member of that body it is improper to speak on issues before the conference. A bishop has no part in making the decision as to who shall and who shall not be admitted as a ministerial member of the conference, nor in the ultimate decision to terminate a minister's relationship to the conference. Despite these limitations and many more, the office is widely regarded as the most powerful in United Methodism.

What is the source of this power? It springs almost entirely from the power of appointment of all ministerial members of the Annual

Conference. Though consultation with the cabinet, the Pastor-Parish Relations Committee, and the person involved is required, the actual appointment is the bishop's prerogative. He or she makes it and bears the responsibility for it. This single fact is the basis of much episcopal power, and explains an influence in many areas of the church's life where, according to the cold print of the *Discipline*, a bishop has no voice at all. Add to this appointive power the responsibility for making certain nominations of personnel for general church boards and agencies and offices, and the basis for episcopal power is pretty well laid.

Actually, United Methodists are agreed on the whole that their bishops need this power and that it is well placed. The appointive system has worked well throughout its history, both for ministers and for churches. While it may sound arbitrary and dictatorial, in actual practice it is not. Most bishops and their cabinets are involved throughout most of the year in the painstaking work of appointment making. This involves countless conferences with individual ministers and with Pastor-Parish Relations Committees. Many false starts are made—that is, bishop and cabinet will leave a meeting thinking they have worked out a set of appointments that will stick; but consultations that take place before they next meet reveal that it won't work, so they must start again from scratch. While such a process is difficult and time-consuming, it finally results in appointments which are likely to be right. And it certainly is a far cry from the myth that appointments are arbitrarily made by the bishop. True, he or she must say the final word and take the final responsibility, but only after a thorough process that has considered the needs of each church and the needs of each minister. More than one minister has said, "I would rather place my future in the hands of a United Methodist bishop and cabinet than anyone I know," and most ministers would agree. The power of appointment is certainly considered a sacred trust and a matter of stewardship by our bishops.

While taking part in programs of the Annual Conference is not listed among the bishops' disciplinary responsibilities, they are often asked to do so, particularly in major evangelistic efforts or major capital funds campaigns. To the extent of time available, bishops almost always respond to such requests favorably, and their leadership inevitably gives added impetus to the entire program. Every bishop also has responsibilities on a general board, agency, or committee and may be chairperson of one. Some of the most important work a bishop does for the general church is in these groups, but this is not always appreciated by the folks back home, who may think (and say), "The bishop is away too much." But this is part of the price we pay for having bishops whom we regard as both general superintendents (having responsibility for the work of the whole church) and resident bishops (having responsibility for the work of a particular area of the church). Actually, much of the strength of our episcopacy comes from this dual nature of the role. Constant touch with the nitty-gritty problems of the local churches of each area helps keep their work on the national level in touch with reality, and their work on the national level helps avoid parochialism.

Bishops elected by the Jurisdictional Conferences are elected for life. They may resign from the office, but this is something that has happened only rarely in our history. Bishops *may* request retirement after twenty years of total ministerial service, including at least four years as an active bishop. However, they would not receive a pension until they reached age sixty-two. The *must* retire at the Jurisdictional Conference if their sixty-sixth birthday occurs prior to the first day of the month in which the conference is held. (Practically speaking, this means a bishop faces mandatory retirement from ages sixty-six to sixty-nine, depending on his or her birthday in relation to the session of the Jurisdictional Conference.) There are also provisions for both voluntary and involuntary retirement for reasons of health.

A retired bishop continues to sit in the Council of Bishops, but without vote. A bishop may be called out of retirement to take temporary responsibility for an episcopal area.

The criticism has sometimes been made of the United Methodist episcopacy that it is too much of an administrative office and not enough of a pastoral office. There is perhaps some validity in such a critique. A bishop, like a pastor of a local church, can become so bogged down in administrative work that there is no

110

time left to be a pastor. Why does a pastor of a church let this happen? It may be because he or she likes administrative work better than pastoral work; or it may be that the expectations of the people for the accomplishment of other things seem so much more pressing than their expectations for pastoral work that the pastor proceeds to do what they expect.

What I am suggesting here is that there is nothing in the office of either a bishop or a pastor which keeps either from being a good pastor to those under him or her. What each needs to do is to give pastoring some priority; and, in each case, the people need to see the value of that priority, and then respect it. Some of our bishops do tremendous pastoral work with the pastors serving under them. Because of their authority role, they may not be able to do everything that an independent counselor might do, but they are also able to do some things which the independent counselor cannot do.

All of this is not to suggest that our United Methodist concept of the episcopacy is perfect, for it is not; there is little question that we should seek for structures that will make the office more of a pastoral one. It is only to suggest that structure is not a guarantee of the desired end result; the will of the officeholder is as of great or greater importance.

The episcopacy has served United Methodism well. Even in the absence of the third Restrictive Rule of our Constitution, United Methodists are not about to do away with episcopacy. Our chief pastors, though not always agreed with, or revered, are almost universally loved and respected. They are worthy bearers of the highest office United Methodism can bestow.

Accountability of Bishop and Superintendent

To whom are bishops and district superintendents accountable? Historically and logically, they are accountable to the entity which chooses them. Thus in the case of district superintendent, accountability is to the bishop. In the case of the bishop, accountability is to the Jurisdictional Conference through its Committee on Episcopacy.

The 1976 General Conference, recognizing the need for additional support systems for both bishop and district superintendent, provided for a conference Committee on Episcopacy and district Committees on the District Superintendency. These committees are intended to be supportive, to provide counsel, and in the case of the Episcopacy Committee, make reports to the Jurisdictional Committee on Episcopacy. These committees are thus not a substitute for existing systems of accountability, but are supplementary to and supportive of them.

Chapter VI

THE CONFERENCES

If the episcopacy is the guarantee of continuity of leadership and administration in The United Methodist Church, the conference system is its guarantee of basic democratic process. Almost all of the personnel decisions in our church are in the hands of the episcopacy, but almost all of the policy decisions are in the hands of the conferences—General, Jurisdictional or Central, Annual, District, and Charge. This chain of conferences represents a chain of representative democracy which permeates and undergirds our entire church.

The General Conference, the "Congress" of United Methodism

The analogy between the General Conference and the Congress of the United States has some validity for us, but some drawbacks as well. Both are representative bodies, and both have a primary responsibility of producing legislation. Both are governed by roughly similar rules of parliamentary procedure, and both do much of their hard work in legislative committees, which then bring their recommendations to the floor. The United States Senate is presided over by a representative of another branch of government (the vice-president), and so it is in the General Conference, with a bishop in the presiding officer's chair. Each day members of Congress are provided with copies of the *Congressional Record*, in which the proceedings of the previous day are printed; members of the General Conference receive similar service in the printing of the *Daily Christian Advocate*. There is also a certain amount of inattention to the immediate proceedings, marked by delegates reading newspapers and the previous day's proceedings, which is common to both bodies! And when recess comes, conversations buzz in the hallways and rest rooms. And the final product of all this in each case is legislation; in the case of the General Conference it is legislation that will constitute the *Discipline* of the church.

But there are important differences as well. For one, the body is not national, but international, with delegates from Annual Conferences in many lands. Another difference is the complete seriousness with which the delegates take their task. This may be due to the fact that they all know they have about ten days in which to do all their work. So they are present at meetings of the legislative committees, and they are present on the floor when the conference is in session; empty sets are a rarity. General Conference delegates, of course, get no pay. They are paid their transportation and a modest *per diem* allowance during the Conference, and they are quite likely to vote down proposals for an increase in their *per diem*!

What about politics at the General Conference? Are there smoke-filled rooms? We could answer that question, "No, United Methodists are not likely to be tobacco users!" But, seriously, there naturally are politics at the General Conference in the sense that delegates, bishops, board secretaries, and other concerned people are doing what they can to convince and persuade other delegates on issues about which they have deep convictions. In recent General Conferences there has been an increase in organized political activity, and in many ways this has been a healthy development, forcing the General Conference to deal with issues which it might otherwise pass by. I would express the hope, however, that such activity would not increase to the point where "parties" would develop within the church. Such a development would surely be destructive to the unity of the church. Politics in the sense of bartering and trading votes is *not* a part of the General Conference scene; at least I have not seen it in five General Conferences in which I have served as a delegate. Perhaps part of the reason for this is sheer lack of time—so much has to be done in so short a time that there is hardly time for politics as it may be practiced in the halls of Congress. But more importantly, delegates regard their votes as matters of sacred responsibility, not to be traded away for political gain. So, though there are many similarities between the General Conference and the Congress of the United States, that are some real differences as well.

The General Conference meets every four years in April or May, and is composed of from six hundred to one thousand delegates, half of whom are ministerial and half lay. The delegates are elected by their Annual Conferences, the number from each conference being determined by a two-factor basis. One factor is the number of ministerial members and the other is the number of church members in the Annual Conference. However, every Annual Conference is entitled to at least one ministerial and one lay delegate, even though it is so small that it would not qualify for any delegates under the formula set forth in Paragraph 602.

In addition to the voting delegates there are some persons who have the privilege of the floor, but no vote. The executive heads of all the boards and agencies of the church have such a privilege in regard to matters affecting their interest. A similar privilege is extended to representatives from Provisional Annual Conferences in matters affecting those particular bodies, as well as to affiliated autonomous Methodist churches.

While bishops have no voice or vote in the General Conference, they are present and one of their number serves as presiding officer. The selection of bishops to be presiding officers is in the hands of a Committee on Presiding Officers made up of lay and ministerial delegates.

The only permanent officer of the General Conference is the secretary, and even this is not a full-time position. He or she is nominated by the Council of Bishops, but there may also be nominations from the floor, with the General Conference then proceeding to the election.

Unlike some of the other bodies of United Methodism which provide that whoever is present in response to a properly called meeting is a quorum, the General Conference has a set

115

quorum—a majority of the whole number of delegates must be present to do business.

One of the democratic guarantees provided in the *Discipline* is the right of any organization, minister, or layperson of The United Methodist Church to submit a petition to the General Conference (Par. 608). Legislative attempts to limit the right of making petitions so that individuals could not make them have failed, the General Conference feeling that the right to petition is so basic that it should not be limited. The result is that thousands of petitions are received by each General Conference on a great variety of subjects. These come from individuals, Sunday school classes, local church commissions or Administrative Boards, Charge Conferences, Annual Conferences, and a whole list of other organizations of our church. Ordinarily, these petitions must be in the hands of the secretary of the General Conference sixty days before the conference opens, and they are then sorted out and assigned to one of the legislative committees of the conference. These petitions then become, in effect, the agenda for the legislative committees; and if there are many petitions, as there usually are, it may require division of the committee into subcommittees and even sub-subcommittees in order to give all of them proper consideration. The legislative committees often have other important agendas to consider, such as proposals growing out of studies carried on during the previous quadrennium. But every petition must be dealt with by the legislative committee, and eventually by the General Conference. While this process is long and arduous, and opens the door for all sorts of alleged crackpots to submit some rather bizarre ideas, it nevertheless serves an important democratic purpose and often provides good ideas that are adopted by the General Conference and become part of the *Discipline.*

Finally, the General Conference possesses the unique privilege of being the only group which can speak officially for The United Methodist Church. Other groups within the church may speak for themselves, and should make this clear when they do speak. But only when the General Conference adopts a position can it properly be said, "The United Methodist Church stands for this" (Par. 610).

Organization and Affiliation Outside the United States

The United Methodist Church began as strictly an American church. But with the coming of the great missionary movement of the nineteenth century, our missionaries went to many places of the world, and often established local churches. As the number of local churches grew in an area, the need for regional organization was felt, such as an Annual Conference. When such Annual Conferences were established, they gained the right to send delegates to the General Conference, and it began to take on an international flavor.

In the early days, the Annual Conferences overseas were presided over by bishops from America. But this kind of absentee leadership was not very effective, and later the Central Conference came into being largely as a means to provide indigenous episcopal leadership. A Central Conference, like a Jurisdictional Conference, is made up of an equal number of lay and ministerial delegates elected from the Annual Conferences. It meets quadrennially, and one of its principal duties is to elect bishops. The Central Conference is given freedom under the Constitution to set the tenure for its bishops, and a number of them provide for a term tenure. The Central Conference is also given a good deal of freedom to adapt disciplinary procedures to the conditions of its area, as long as it does not violate the Constitution or the General Rules (Par. 638.9). In general, the concept of the Central Conference is to give maximum freedom to the church in an overseas area while still retaining it within our structure.

However, the growth of nationalism and the desire for independence have led many portions of the church in other lands to seek the status of an affiliated autonomous church. When this is desired, certain procedures (Par. 649) must be followed, leading to an actual severing of ties with The United Methodist Church, except by affiliation. This affiliation gives the church the right to send nonvoting delegates to the General Conference, and provides for the right to transfer members and ministers between the churches.

While movement toward autonomy seemed very much in favor

117

a few years ago, the present mood seems to be one of reassessment of the value of being an integral part of a worldwide structure. In fact, the 1980 General Conference, in response to wishes expressed by some autonomous churches, adopted for the first time legislation providing for autonomous churches to become a part of The United Methodist Church if they so desired (Par. 653). Thorough studies of the future relationships within world United Methodism are continuing.

The Jurisdictional Conference

In chapter 1 we considered the Jurisdictional Conference briefly, indicating a bit of its history, the fact that it is established in five regions within the United States, and that its principal task is electing bishops.

How valid is the jurisdictional system? For those who interpreted its original rationale as being solely a way to provide for a segregated structure for black churches and Annual Conferences, the rationale is gone with the abolition of the Central Jurisdiction. The only rationale which remains is the principle of regionalism. How valid is that principle? Those who favor it would point to the fact that regions of the country differ politically, sociologically, and in their church life, and therefore they should have the chance to plan their programs and elect their bishops in the light of their own needs. They might also point to the democratic principle that groups ought to be able to elect their own leaders, with a maximum participation by the people who are going to be led in the selection of who will lead them. Opponents of the jurisdictional system and regionalism tend to feel that regionalism is synonymous with parochialism. They also feel that election of bishops by the General Conference would ensure that the bishops are the choice of the whole church and reflect its values, rather than being persons who might suit the prejudices of a particular region. They might point to our tradition which regards bishops as "general superintendents," bishops of the whole church, and thus properly elected by the whole church.

The argument for the system based on regional differences is not

118

too compelling, as modern media are constantly diminishing the extent and importance of regional disparity. The argument for a more democratic participation in the election of bishops is a stronger one, since the jurisdictional system does provide for a wider and more direct participation in the selection of leadership by those over whom the leader will serve. If we carried this to its extreme, we would follow the system of the Episcopal Church and each conference or area would elect its own bishop, but in the United Methodist tradition of the general superintendency, this would be going too far and would undoubtedly promote parochialism. Furthermore, this would violate the United Methodist appointive system by allowing a constituency to elect and call its own "pastor," rather than having one appointed to it. Election of bishops by the General Conference has some theoretical validity, but the growth in the number of bishops and the large number to be elected each General Conference would result in an extremely unwieldly process, and one very far removed from the people directly concerned. All in all, it seems that the jurisdictional system strikes a reasonable balance between the parochialism of more local election of bishops on the one hand, and the rather undemocratic remoteness of election by the General Conference on the other. It would appear that the jurisdictions, or something like them, are here to stay.

The Annual Conference

If the General Conference is the Congress of United Methodism, then the Annual Conference is its state legislature. The analogy is quite a rough one, but it gives some idea of the relationships involved.

The Constitution refers to the Annual Conference as the "basic body in the Church." This reference is partly historical, but partly refers to some of the key powers which the Annual Conference possesses. Among these are the right to vote on all constitutional amendments, the right of election of the delegates to the General Conference, and the right to determine all matters concerning ordination, character, and conference relations of ministers. This

119

last right is actually exercised not by the entire Annual Conference, but by the ministerial members in full connection.

The Annual Conference membership is composed of its ministerial members (those in full connection, probationary, associate members, and full-time local pastors under appointment) and lay members. Ministers in full connection have the right to vote on all matters before the Annual Conference except the election of lay delegates to the General and Jurisdictional Conferences. Probationary and associate members and full-time local pastors under appointment have the right to vote on all matters except the election of lay or ministerial delegates to the General and Jurisdictional Conferences, constitutional amendments, and all matters of ordination, character, and conference relations of ministers. The lay members have the right to vote on all matters except the election of ministerial delegates to the General and Jurisdictional Conferences, and all matters of ordination, character, and conference relations of ministers.

Also certain persons are members of the Annual Conference by virtue of their office. These are the conference president of United Methodist Women, the conference president of United Methodist Men, the conference lay leader, the president of the conference youth organization, and two young persons under twenty-five from each district to be selected in whatever manner the Annual Conference determines. Diaconal ministers are now voting lay members. Furthermore, the lay equalization amendment to the Constitution adopted during the 1972-76 quadrennium gives each Annual Conference the right to provide additional lay members by whatever plan it may determine, in order to provide a number of lay members equal to ministerial members. In addition, there are a number of persons who are not members and who do not have the right to vote, but who have a seat and the privilege of the floor. These are less than full-time local pastors serving a pastoral charge, lay missionaries of the church from fields outside the United States, and official representatives from other denominations.

All members of the conference, lay and ministerial, are required to attend its sessions or else explain their absence in a letter to the conference secretary. If ministers do not attend and have no satisfactory reason for their absence, their names are to be referred to the Board of Ordained Ministry. What the Board of Ordained Ministry does then is not indicated in the *Discipline!*

The date for holding Annual Conference are set by the bishop, but the place is set by the Annual Conference or its committee. However, the bishop and superintendents have the power to change the place if it is necessary. Special sessions may be called in two ways: by the Annual Conference after consulting with the bishop, or by the bishop if three-fourths of the superintendents agree to it. Such a special session can act only on the matters specified in the call.

The Annual Conference has power to adopt rules and regulations as long as they are not in conflict with the *Discipline.* For instance, an Annual Conference may adopt stricter requirements for ministerial membership than those provided in the *Discipline,* but it may not adopt lesser requirements. Furthermore, the conference has the power to inquire into financial deficits and membership problems of local churches and to require that the pastor and lay member appear before an appropriate committee to discuss the matter.

The conference business consists largely of hearing the reports and acting on the recommendations of the various boards and agencies of the conference. It also includes election of personnel to the various boards and agencies, and the adoption of conference budgets for the year. A Communion service is traditional in most conferences, with regular devotional services throughout the conference time. The service of ordination and a final service ending with the reading of the appointments for the next year are traditional, although some bishops are now reading the appointments early in the conference on the theory that this relieves tension!

The Annual Conference is different things to different people. There are some members who feel it is dry, boring, and a waste of time and money. But the majority of lay and ministerial members find the sessions exciting and often inspirational, a real exercise in participatory democracy. It is true that sometimes a few of the

121

ministers do most of the talking on the floor of the conference, but this need not be the case when members of the conference, lay and ministerial, make it their business to become knowledgeable on issues before them and on matters of procedure.

The conference functions through a fairly large number of boards and agencies. The following conference agencies are mandated by the *Discipline*: Council on Finance and Administration, Commission on Equitable Salaries, Council on Ministries, Board of Higher Education and Campus Ministry, Board of Ordained Ministry, Board of Diaconal Ministry, Committee on Episcopacy, Board of Pensions, Commission on Archives and History, Commission on Christian Unity and Interreligious Concerns, Commission on Religion and Race, Commission on the Status and Role of Women, Joint Committee on Disability, Joint Review Committee, and Committee on Investigation. In addition, the three major program boards of the church (Church and Society, Discipleship and Global Ministries) *may* be organized at the Annual Conference level, but if not, must have their functions assigned to a responsible conference body. Only three structures are mandatory at the district level: the District Committee on Ordained Ministry, the Committee on District Superintendency, and the Board of Church Location and Building.

While most of these agencies will be described elsewhere in these pages, one of them is so uniquely related to the Annual Conference that this seems the appropriate place to describe it. The Board of Ordained Ministry is an extremely important board in each Annual Conference which is concerned with the ministers of the conference from the cradle to the grave. That may be a slight exaggeration, but it is concerned and charged with responsibility from the time a young person may first exhibit interest in the ministry until retirement and even beyond. This board is made up entirely of ministerial members in full connection. The bishop actually makes the nominations of members for the Board of Ordained Ministry after consultation with the outgoing chairperson of the board for the previous quadrennium and with the cabinet. This is in contrast with the other boards and agencies of the conference, practically all of which have their members nominated by a conference nominating committee. Thus, the bishop is provided an indirect but important way to influence the whole area of ministerial relationships.

These are some of the responsibilities the Board of Ordained Ministry carries: recruiting men and women for the ministry; screening and testing candidates at all levels of progress; administering scholarships and other funds received through the Ministerial Education Fund apportionment; developing continuing education programs; providing resources to help ministers deal with problems of the ministry; interviewing and making recommendations concerning all ministers who are seeking to leave the ministry or seeking another relationship, including retirement; plus other duties which the Annual Conference may place upon it! The great brunt of this voluminous work load falls upon the registrar of the board, who must keep files on every candidate in process. At any given time in the average Annual Conference this involves scores of active files, and the registrar, who is almost always doing this work as a labor of love, is truly one of the unsung heroes in the Annual Conference structure.

The Board of Ordained Ministry is assisted in its work by the district Committee on Ordained Ministry. It is made up of a representative from the Board of Ordained Ministry, named by the board in consultation with the superintendent; five ministers in full connection of the district nominated by the superintendent in consultation with the chairperson of the board or its executive committee; and the district superintendent. The member from the board *may* be the committee chairperson, and the superintendent *may* be the executive secretary. Presumably, the committee is free to elect its own officers. This group especially concerns itself with interviewing and certifying candidates for the ministry, but it also is charged with making recommendations to the Board of Ordained Ministry concerning several other matters of ministerial status.

PROVISIONAL ANNUAL CONFERENCES, MISSIONARY CONFERENCES, MISSIONS, AND DISTRICT CONFERENCES. An Annual Conference must ordinarily have at least fifty ministerial members in full connection in order to be and continue as an Annual Conference (Par. 25.4). Sometimes, however, it seems desirable to create a structure like an Annual Conference, even with a smaller number of ministers. If there are ten or more ministers available, a Provisional Annual Conference may be organized. Such a development usually takes place on a mission field where the general growth in the scope of the work warrants it. A Provisional Conference has most of the powers of a regular Annual Conference, but may not elect delegates to the General Conference. If the ministerial membership of the conference declines below six, it cannot continue in this status.

A Missionary Conference is also organized in the same manner as an Annual Conference, but because of limited personnel and resources requires substantial aid and administrative guidance from the Board of Global Ministries. Such a conference would function as an Annual Conference with certain exceptions. The question of status of a minister who is a member both of an Annual Conference and a Missionary Conference as clarified by the 1976 General Conference, providing for an affiliate membership in the Missionary Conference.

A Mission does not purport to be an Annual Conference in any sense, but functions more like a District Conference (Par. 663). Ministerial members serving in the Mission actually continue to hold their conference membership back home in an Annual Conference, from which they receive appointments as missionaries. The Board of Global Ministries is deeply involved in both the administration and support of Missions, but the bishop in charge appoints the superintendent and makes the appointments of preachers to their charges.

District Conferences are an optional structure utilized in some Annual Conferences which desire them. The District Conference is made up in a manner to be determined by the Annual Conference. The only actual power it has is to vote on issuing certificates of candidacy for the ministry on recommendation of the district Committee on Ordained Ministry. This lack of authority may be one reason this structure is not widely used in United Methodism.

The Charge Conference

Because the Charge Conference was discussed at length in an earlier chapter on the local church, only brief mention will be made here. But it is important to place the Charge Conference in its context as the last in the chain of conferences which are a guarantee of the democratic process in United Methodism at all levels. There is a very real sense in which the entire conference system of our church rests ultimately on the shoulders of every individual member of The United Methodist Church. For every member has a vote in the Church Conference (Par. 248), and helps elect one or more lay members to the Annual Conference. The lay members, in turn, vote in the election of the lay delegates to the Jurisdictional and the General Conferences. On the ministerial side, no person may become a member without receiving a recommendation from his or her local Charge Conference or Church Conference. Thus, members of the local church exert some control, though admittedly remote, over who the future ministerial members of the Annual Conference, and in turn the Jurisdictional and General Conferences, will be.

Judged by the "one person, one vote" principle, the conference system is far from ideal. However, given the peculiar needs of representation of local churches, both large and small, in the Annual Conference, and the needs of representation of Annual Conferences, both large and small, in the Jurisdictional and General Conferences, it is a remarkably practical, efficient, and democratic means for the basic governance of our church.

Chapter VII

ADMINISTRATIVE STRUCTURES

If someone had a complaint, and wanted to go to the head of The United Methodist Church with it, that head person would be hard to find. One might try the president of the Council of Bishops, but would discover that this person is primarily a presiding officer over the semi-annual meetings of the Council of Bishops. The president has no particular authority in the church at large other than that possessed by all the bishops, and certainly has no actual authority over the other bishops.

One might try the general secretary of the General Council on Ministries, but would discover that this person, though head of an agency involved in coordinating the total work of the program agencies of the church, is by no means in charge of the total work of The United Methodist Church. If our complainant went to see the executive head of one of our boards or agencies, he or she would be told that that person has charge of only a certain portion of the work of the church. One might approach the presiding bishop of a session of the General Conference, but would be told that anywhere from fifteen to twenty-five bishops may share in the task of presiding at any quadrennial meeting of the General Conference. If one were to go to the president of the Judicial Council, he or she would be told, "All we do is decide cases."

President Harry Truman used to have a motto on his desk which read, "The buck stops here." There is really no single desk in

United Methodism which can appropriately display that motto. If it can be placed anywhere in the church, it would have to be on the nine hundred or more desks of the delegates to the General Conference during their approximately ten-day session once every four years. They have the authority to eliminate every structure, board, and agency within the entire church except those with constitutional status, such as the episcopacy, the district superintendency, the conferences, and the Judicial Council.

This is simply to illustrate the fact that power and authority are widely dispersed within The United Methodist Church, undoubtedly deliberately so. We have inherited from the founders of America a rather keen distrust of too much power centralized in one person. There is not only not a head person, there are no headquarters of our church! This is not necessarily bad, but we should recognize that this general lack of central direction over the years has resulted in our various boards and agencies pretty much going their own independent ways, each developing its own programs which sometimes overlapped with programs of our other agencies and sometimes actually conflicted with them. The end result is a situation where our total resources are not always put to the best use, and where passing the buck becomes inordinately easy to do.

Attempts have been made to improve the picture. In the former Methodist Church a massive professional study was carried on in the 1948-52 quadrennium, but not many of its recommendations were adopted. One of the reasons the General Conference is often reluctant to vote for reforms is that most of its members are also members of the boards and agencies to be reformed, and they tend to have a kind of vested interest in the *status quo*. This may point to a need for a change in our structure that would rule out dual membership in a board or agency and in the General Conference, even as dual membership in the Judicial Council and the General Conference is not now permitted. This would be a drastic move and a highly debatable one, but the clear need for a more effective authority over the boards and agencies seems quite evident, and the General Conference must be willing to act responsibly.

Progress is definitely being made. The action of the 1972

127

General Conference in establishing a General Council on Ministries is the most far-reaching yet taken to provide true accountability to the whole church. The General Council on Ministries has moved forward in an effective and responsible way to bring an essential unit into our denominational programming, but its role continues to be debated.

When the Jews left or fled from Israel and dispersed to all parts of the earth, this was known as the diaspora. In The United Methodist Church we have a kind of administrative diaspora with which we are quite comfortable because of the way it disperses power, but many United Methodists are wondering how much longer we can afford it. This may account for increasing calls for the Council of Bishops to assume more leadership.

Structures of General Agencies

The general agencies of our church are defined in Paragraph 801 as being the "regularly established councils, boards, commissions, or committees which have been constituted by the General Conference." Thus, the general agencies do not include constitutionally established agencies such as the Council of Bishops and the Judicial Council. Neither do they include committees created by the General Conference for a special task during a quadrennium, ecumenical groups on which The United Methodist Church is represented, nor any of the committees related to the session of the General Conference.

Persons may not serve as members of more than one agency (with certain exceptions). A person cannot be a chairperson of more than one agency or a division of it, and staff members of agencies are not eligible to be members of any agency, nor are any persons who receive compensation from it. Furthermore, there is an eight-year tenure rule which means that this is the limit of time any member can serve consecutively as an agency member. Members elected from Jurisdictions give up their membership if they move to another Jurisdiction.

All the agencies are basically amenable to the General Conference. In the interim between General Conferences, the program agencies are accountable to the Council on Ministries, and all agencies are required to cooperate with the Council on Ministries. They have no special relationship to the episcopacy, although every agency has one or more bishops in its membership, and some may elect a bishop as president or chairperson. This places considerable authority in the hands of the bishops, and serves as an informal means of correlation of agencies through the bishops' association with one another in the Council of Bishops and other places.

Attempts to classify the agencies are rather difficult, and can never be absolutely clear-cut, but for the purposes of this chapter I will classify them under three categories: Agencies for Administration, Support Service Agencies, and Program Agencies. Under this classification, Agencies for Administration are those which have a responsibility for oversight of the work of the church or certain aspects of it; Support Service Agencies are primarily involved with serving the needs of the church in order to make it possible to carry out its mission; and Program Agencies are those primarily involved in carrying out the mission of the church through preaching, teaching, and action.

Agencies for administration

COUNCIL OF BISHOPS. This is a constitutionally established agency of the church, made up of all the bishops, including those who are retired, who have a voice but no vote. It ordinarily meets semi-annually to carry out its responsibilities, which are described in the Constitution a follows: to "plan for the general oversight and promotion of the temporal and spiritual interests of the entire Church and for carrying into effect the rules, regulations, and responsibilities prescribed and enjoined by the General Conference." One way of getting some idea of the heavy load which this involves is to look in the index of the *Discipline* under "Council of Bishops" and see the amazing number of references listed there to a wide assortment of tasks which the church places in their hands.

Not only does the council carry out these many administrative tasks, but the bishops serve as "chief pastors" and have the

129

responsibility for expressing and implementing the pastoral concern of the whole church, even as a pastor does with the local congregation. Thus the Council of Bishops serves an indispensable function for the whole church as it carries out its constitutional duties.

GENERAL COUNCIL ON MINISTRIES. This structure, created by the 1972 General Conference, is intended to be responsible, between sessions of the General Conference, for the total program of The United Methodist Church. It does this through its power to review and ensure the development of a unified and coordinated ongoing program, to change priorities in concurrence with the Council of Bishops as needs emerge between sessions of the General Conference (as long as this is done within the total budget authorized by the General Conference), to eliminate overlapping functions of boards and agencies, to engage in research and planning, and to make proposals to the General Conference for emphases and priorities. The exact limits of its powers over boards and agencies will probably only emerge as it functions, but there is no question of the intent of the General Conference to create a far more powerful body at this level than the church has ever had before. The church, through the creation of this structure, seemed to be saying that it was tired of practically autonomous boards and agencies who seemed to be accountable to no one.

The Council on Ministries is made up of about 120 persons, the bulk of whom are representatives of each Annual Conference within the United States. That is, each Annual Conference nominates one layman, one laywoman, and one clergy to the Jurisdictional Conference. From these the Jurisdictional Conference elects one person from each Annual Conference in such a way that the total from the jurisdiction will be one-third laymen, one-third laywomen, and one-third clergy. One of the clergy shall be a woman. Six bishops are also members, one from each jurisdiction and one from outside the United States, selected by the Council of Bishops. One youth and one young adult are elected from each jurisdiction, and each program board or commission is entitled to one non-staff, non-episcopal representative. Three persons from Central Conferences are also members, plus fifteen members at large elected by the council in order to ensure ethnic representation.

Members are elected to four-year terms, with a maximum tenure of eight years. A general secretary is elected annually.

Provision is also made for an optional Jurisdictional Council on Ministries and a mandatory Annual Conference Council on Ministries.

The General Council on Ministries has its headquarters in Dayton, Ohio.

GENERAL COUNCIL ON FINANCE AND ADMINISTRATION. This is the top fiscal control body of The United Methodist Church, and as such it carries a tremendous responsibility in the handling of huge sums of money. The council is composed of forty-two members, including three bishops. None of the members, including the bishops, may be members of or employed by any general agency of the church. The council elects a general secretary, who is also the treasurer of the council. The major responsibility of the council is the preparing of a quadrennial budget for the entire United Methodist Church at the national level. This involves holding hearings in which all the agencies present their proposed budgets, estimates of possible income, and finally coming up with a budget for action by the General Conference. However, all World Service agencies will have their proposed budgets determined by the Council on Ministries within a total budget approved by the Council on Finance and Administration, with the provision that before all budgets are finalized they are to be jointly approved by the two councils. Once a budget is adopted, the council must adopt procedures to see that the money is handled efficiently and spent wisely.

The Council on Finance and Administration requires periodic audit of all the agencies receiving funds from it, and has a responsibility to search out cases of overlapping activities of agencies and to call this to the attention of the agencies. It then has a responsibility to work the problem out with the agencies, and may, in consultation with and approval of the Council on

131

Ministries, decline to release funds if the matter is not properly resolved. The council also pays the salaries and expenses of the bishops, and carries out extensive property and management functions on behalf of most of the agencies of the church, and holds title to certain properties on behalf of the entire church.

In each Annual Conference there is a Council on Finance and Administration, composed of five to twenty-one persons, divided one-third laymen, one-third laywomen, and one-third clergy. These persons may not be members or employees of any agency that receives funds from the Annual Conference. They perform on the conference level basically what the general council does on the national level, although the budgets must be prepared every year. This involves considering the various agencies and causes and establishing budgets for submission to the Annual Conference. The council nominates a conference treasurer for election by the conference to serve as the executive officer of the council. The council has the hard job of endeavoring to collect the various apportionments from the local churches. The district superintendents are of great assistance at this point, and the pastor is almost always deeply concerned that when the fiscal year comes to an end, local church apportionments are paid in full.

The General Council on Finance and Administration and the conference councils, then, are the tough-minded watchdogs of our dollars, and we are grateful for their practical service to the church.

The council has its headquarters in Evanston, Illinois.

Support Service Agencies

GENERAL BOARD OF PUBLICATION. The Board of Publication, or as it and its entire operation are usually referred to, The United Methodist Publishing House, enjoys the distinction of being the oldest continuing enterprise of the church, since it originated in 1789. This board is also unique in that it is the only board whose principal task is the operation of a multimillion-dollar manufacturing, publishing, distribution, and retail establishment. The fifty-member board is composed of two bishops, ten members at large elected by the board, and thirty-eight persons elected by the

132

Jurisdictional Conferences, representing as nearly as possible an equal number of ministers and laypersons.

The board elects an executive whose title is president and publisher. He is responsible for the entire operation and in turn is responsible to the board. The board also elects a book editor, who is responsible with the publisher for the approving of all manuscripts for publication and for supervising the editing of all our books, along with the periodical *Quarterly Review*. When requested by other agencies, the book editor collaborates with editors of their publications, but does not bear responsibility for their content.

The Board of Publication occupies a unique place among the agencies of the church. It is responsible for a large business operation, The United Methodist Publishing House, which is self-sustaining and provides revenue to the church for the support of its pension program for ministers. This status gives it certain privileges which other agencies do not have, such as the freedom to buy property and build buildings without prior clearance with the Council on Ministries, as is required of all other agencies. Because of this special place, and because other agencies of the church rely on this board for their printing, it is particularly vulnerable to criticism. This means that this board, which performs such an immense service to the whole church, must also bear a special measure of responsibility for its operation as an arm of The United Methodist Church.

The Board of Publication has its headquarters in Nashville, Tennessee.

GENERAL BOARD OF PENSIONS. This thirty-member board of ministers and laypersons is responsible for the entire pension program of The United Methodist Church. This is a complicated and very responsible task, involving the handling of millions of dollars in investments and the careful compiling of records of service of thousands of personnel of the church. To carry out this work, a general secretary is elected, along with such other staff as is necessary. The staff works closely with the Annual Conference Boards of Pensions, each of which may have slightly differing pension programs and needs. One of the functions of the board is to

133

serve as a clearinghouse, so that a minister who has served in three to four different Annual Conferences during a lifetime doesn't have to worry about collecting several pensions, but collects one for which the board has allocated responsibility according to years of service.

The General Board of Pensions relies quite heavily on the Annual Conference Board of Pensions, a mandatory body in each Annual Conference, to carry out certain important responsibilities. It is the conference board which must recommend to the Annual Conference ways to raise money to fund the pension program, and must recommend the annuity rate to be paid. It has the responsibility of ascertaining which years of service are to be approved for pension, according to a disciplinary formula (Par. 1606.3). This Annual Conference board is composed of at least twelve members, divided equally between clergy and laity.

The pension for ministers in our church varies from conference to conference, but it is recommended that the annuity rate be "not less than 1 percent of the average salary of the conference." This means that in a conference where the average salary is $20,000, the rate should be $200, meaning that the minister's annual pension there would be $200 times the years of service. Some Annual Conferences are able to meet this recommended rate, but others are not. Since January 1, 1982, a new "defined contribution" system of pensions has been in effect.

Because the ministry is among the lower paid professions, the existence of a well-ordered pension system is really essential. We can be grateful for the work which our Board of Pensions does, both at the national and the conference level, to provide such a system.

The general board has its headquarters in Evanston, Illinois.

UNITED METHODIST COMMUNICATIONS. This is a new structure created by the 1972 General Conference, originally related to the Council on Ministries, and originally known as the Joint Committee on Communications. Its membership is spelled out in Paragraph 1907, and is now the General Commission on Communications.

The purpose of United Methodist Communications is to help

meet the communication needs of the church and to be the official news-gathering and distributing agency for the church and its general boards and agencies, with consultative relationships to church agencies at all levels. It is authorized to elect a general secretary. The headquarters of this agency is in Nashville, Tennessee.

GENERAL COMMISSION ON ARCHIVES AND HISTORY. This thirty-member commission is the official historical agency of the church. Presided over by a bishop, the commission is made up of ex-officio members, members elected by the General Conference, and nine members at large elected by the commission. A general secretary and other staff may be elected. One of the tasks of this commission is the establishing of archives, into which all official documents, minutes, correspondence and papers of all bishops, general church officers, agencies, committees, and other groups shall be deposited "when they no longer have operational usefulness" (Par. 1811.3b). If this is actually carried out, it would seem that a big increase in staff would be needed to handle the volume! This commission also has the task of making recommendations to the General Conference concerning all national historical shrines, landmarks, and sites.

Optional jurisdictional commissions are provided for, and mandatory Annual Conference commissions, which are to carry out the historical functions at that level.

The headquarters of the commission are at Madison, New Jersey.

Program Agencies

GENERAL BOARD OF CHURCH AND SOCIETY. As its name implies, this board is concerned with relating the gospel of Jesus Christ to the society in which we live. In doing this, it feels called to give forthright leadership and witness and to speak its convictions to the church and the world, recognizing the freedom and responsibility of all Christians to make their decisions on these matters according to their own Christian calling. To do this task effectively means that the board is often involved in controversial issues, and sometimes is in trouble with other segments of the church; but United Methodists recognize that applying the gospel to all of life always results in controversy, and they willingly live with it, rather than take the cowardly alternative of backing away from controversy. The United Methodist Church believes that if the gospel has any validity at all, it has validity for every area of life, and it charges the Board of Church and Society with responsibility to apply the gospel to the most pressing social concerns of our time, and let the chips fall where they may.

The board is made up in the manner established for all program boards, which involves a nominating process going back to the Annual Conferences. Each Annual Conference, on nomination from its General and Jurisdictional Conference delegation, sends nominations to the Jurisdictional Conference. It is to send at least fifteen nominations of persons from eight categories, from one to five in each category. The categories are: clergy, laywomen, laymen, racial and ethnic minority (including at least one Asian-American, one Black American, one Hispanic American, and one Native American), youth, young adult, older adult, and persons with a handicapping condition. From this pool of names the Jurisdictional Conference must select its basic membership of the various General Boards. That membership must be made up of one-third laywomen, one-third laymen, and one-third clergy, including at least one clergywoman. They must also ensure adequate representation of youth and young adults, and are urged to have at least 25 percent of the total from ethnic minorities. They are also to give "special attention" to persons with handicapping conditions. By the time jurisdictional members struggle with this for a few days, they learn how almost impossibly complicated it all is. We have made heroic efforts to ensure inclusiveness in our boards, but surely we can improve on our procedures in the future.

In addition, the Council of Bishops names five to ten bishops to each board, and each board can elect from five to twelve additional members.

The board and its divisions are headquartered in Washington, D.C., but it also maintains a United Nations office which falls under the responsibility of the Division of World Peace.

There is provision in the *Discipline* for an optional jurisdictional board and an optional Annual Conference board. In the event a conference determines not to have a board, it must provide through its Council on Ministries ways to maintain connectional relationships.

GENERAL BOARD OF DISCIPLESHIP. This board, newly created in 1972, is an attempt to bring together under one umbrella all the general church agencies serving the local church. Prior to the 1972 restructuring, at least four separate general agencies sought to serve the local church, and the result was often a confusing, overlapping, and sometimes conflicting situation for the local pastor to whom mailings came from the various agencies. The theory behind this newly created board is to reduce such confusion as much as possible.

The makeup of the board is the same as for all program boards (set forth under the Board of Church and Society). The Board has responsibility for education, evangelism, worship, stewardship, and ministry of the laity, and also has a Division of United Methodist Men.

The total Christian educational program of The United Methodist Church for use in local churches will be developed by the Board for incorporation into the total church program, and is intended to include all educational emphases of the church.

The Board has the responsibility of interpreting and spreading through the church all of the rich meanings of the universal priesthood of believers, of Christian vocation, and of the ministry of the laity. In carrying this out, the division will work with and provide resources for various auxiliary groups in the church, such as the various levels of the United Methodist Youth Ministry. It also has a function of providing resources for Pastor-Parish Relations Committees, Administrative Boards, Charge Conferences, Boards of Trustees, Nominations and Personnel Committees, Committees on Lay Personnel, and those who serve as lay leaders and lay members of Annual Conferences. The division is also concerned with the lay speaker program. The 1988 General Conference created a new Division of United Methodist Men.

137

The Curriculum Resources Committee is responsible for developing curriculum for the educational program of the church.

Administratively related to the Board of Discipleship is the United Methodist National Youth Ministry Organization. This functions through two units: a National Youth Ministry Convocation, which meets biennially in a mass assembly, an NYMO Legislative Assembly made up of three representatives (two youth and one adult from each Annual Conference), and a National Youth Ministry Steering Committee, made up of youth elected by Jurisictional Convocations, plus a bishop and staff members from various boards and agencies, and one Annual Conference adult worker with youth from each Jurisdiction. The Steering Committee is the continuing responsible group, carrying on work related to youth. One of its duties is administering the Youth Service Fund, which is divided 30 percent to the council and 70 percent to Annual Conference Councils on Youth Ministry.

There are optional provisions for Boards of Discipleship at both the jurisdictional and Annual Conference levels.

The Board of Discipleship has its headquarters in Nashville, Tennessee.

GENERAL BOARD OF GLOBAL MINISTRIES. In the restructuring of 1972, this board assumed the function of the former Board of Missions, as well as the functions of the former Commission on Ecumenical Affairs and the Board of Health and Welfare Ministries. The membership of the board is made up basically in the same manner as provided for all other program boards, with the exception that the Women's Division is separately constituted of predominantly women, with the result that the total board membership is approximately 50 percent laywomen, 25 percent clergy, and 25 percent laymen.

This board, one of the largest and strongest in the church, carries out its work through three divisions and four departments.

The National Division has the responsibility for extending the mission of the church in the United States and its dependencies— what used to be called "home missions." Some of the important

138

areas of work included within this division are church estension, field service and finance, urban ministries, town and country ministries architectural services, and so forth.

The Women's Division is composed of about seventy members, of whom sixty are women, plus ten members at large. This division is responsible for a whole program of mission which is supported by the local units of United Methodist Women throughout the church. The division is involved with "the concerns and responsibilities of the Church in today's world, . . . the needs of women and children, . . . and . . . activities which foster growth in the Christian faith, mission education, and Christian social involvement throughout the organization." The Women's Division provides major financial undergirding for the work of the National and World Divisions.

The World Division is concerned with the work of extending the mission of the church in all areas of the world outside the United States and its dependencies. Its concern is with what was called in an earlier day "foreign missions."

The Health and Welfare Ministries Department has an advisory relationship to all hospitals, homes, and similar agencies related to The United Methodist Church. Its purpose is to bring about a holistic view of health care within The United Methodist Church.

The Mission Education and Cultivation Department has the broad task of undergirding the total program of the General Board of Global Ministries with education and cultivation, by communicating and interpreting an understanding of the mission of the church, and by encouraging the giving of funds to the cause.

The Mission Personnel Resources Department is responsible for the personnel functions of the General Board of Global Ministries. This group is also to cooperate with the Office of Career Planning and Personnel Services of the Board of Higher Education and Ministry.

The United Methodist Committee on Relief has the status of a department within the board. It is the function of UMCOR to provide relief for human suffering wherever it may occur, especially in the wake of great disasters. Because it carries out so much of this work through already existing church agencies, it is able to get help to people in need with a minimum of overhead. A large part of its funds come through the One Great Hour of Sharing offering, although it can initiate special appeals for funds to meet an emergency with the approval of the Council of Bishops and the Council on Finance and Administration.

Finally the creation of a General Board of Global Ministries at the jurisdictional level is left optional. The Annual Conference is to have a Board of Global Ministries or "equivalent structure." The Board of Global Ministries has its headquarters in New York City.

GENERAL BOARD OF HIGHER EDUCATION AND MINISTRY. The purpose of this board is to prepare and assist persons in fulfilling their ministry in Christ as this has been historically understood by United Methodism and to provide general oversight and care for our institutions of higher learning. The membership of this board is constituted in the same manner as the other program boards. It is basically the former Board of Education with two divisions related to the local church removed and placed in the Board of Discipleship, and with the addition of the functions formerly carried out by the Commission on Chaplains. The board functions through four divisions.

The Division of Higher Education maintains an advisory relationship with schools, colleges, and universities of our church, and makes studies and gives approval for any new institutions which may desire United Methodist relationship. The division also is concerned with efforts to establish a campus Christian movement and a ministry to the educational ommunity. It is committed to an ecumenical approach to this task, although some of this work is still carried on through the denominational Wesley Foundations as well. The Office of Loans and Scholarships administers an extensive loan and scholarship program for United Methodist college students, using funds received from United Methodist Student Day offerings as well as other sources.

Closely related to the Division of Higher Education is the University Senate, which is the accrediting and standardizing agency for all the educational institutions of the church. It is made up of twenty-five persons who are not members of the Board of Higher Education and Ministry, picked for their training and experience in the work of establishing standards and evaluating educational institutions. The associate general secretary of the Division of Higher Education serves as the executive secretary of this body. This agency is one of the oldest and most distinguished in the church, having pioneered in the whole matter of accreditation of institutions of higher learning in the United States.

The Division of Ordained Ministry is involved at the national level with all the concerns of Annual Conference Boards of Ordained Ministry as spelled out in chapter 6. This involves recruitment, guidance, training, qualifications, courses of study, conference relations of ministers, continuing education, and relationships with all the seminaries of the church, as well as ecumenical involvements. The expanded view of this office which came with the Methodist-E.U.B. union has greatly increased the scope of this division to include practically the whole life of the ordained minister.

The Division of Chaplains and Related Ministries has a dual responsibility. The first is administrative, in that it serves as the recruiting, endorsing, and general overseeing arm of the church for all our chaplains in the military and institutional work of all kinds. Once recruited and endorsed by this division for a particular chaplaincy, a chaplain is then kept in touch with the church by the division and aided in every possible way in this task. A second responsibility is to help provide a ministry to persons in the armed forces and in institutions, and to help local churches and other groups do the same.

The Division of Diaconal Ministry is concerned with studying needs and setting standards for career workers within the church who are not ordained.

Organization of the Board of Higher Education and Ministry is optional at the jurisdictional level, but an Annual Conference Board of Higher Education and Campus Ministry is mandatory.

The Board has its headquarters in Nashville, Tennessee.

GENERAL COMMISSION ON CHRISTIAN UNITY AND INTERRELIGIOUS CONCERNS. This commission has the task of proclaiming and working for the unity of the whole of Christ's church. It is composed of some forty members, with twenty elected by jurisdictions, twelve members at large, four bishops, and two members from other member denominations of the Consultation on Church Union. The Commission carries responsibility for the total ecumenical stance and work of the church, recommends to the Council of Bishops persons to serve on ecumenial groups, and serves as a liaison between these groups and the church. This commission and its staff bear a special relationship to the Council of Bishops, since the Council officially represents the denomination in relations with other denominations. This Commission is also responsible for relationships with representatives of non-Christian religions.

The commission has its headquarters in New York City.

GENERAL COMMISSION ON RELIGION AND RACE. This commission, formerly a temporary quadrennial commission, became permanent in 1972. It is made up of forty-eight members, with a strong representation of ethnic minority groups. In general, its task is to assist in every way the cause of empowerment of ethnic minorities, including working with non-church-related groups involved in the same cause. Furthermore, it has a major educational task in the area of racism and racist attitudes. Provision is also made for an Annual Conference commission.

The commission has its headquarters in Washington, D. C.

GENERAL COMMISSION ON THE STATUS AND ROLE OF WOMEN. This group, made permanent by the 1976 General Conference, is made up of forty-eight members, a majority of whom are women and whose president is to be a woman. It is charged with responsibility "to challenge The United Methodist Church . . . to a continuing commitment to the full and equal responsibility and participation of women in the total life and mission of the Church."

Provision is also made for an Annual Conference Commission or other comparably structured unit.

The commission has its headquarters in Evanston, Illinois.

142

Ecumenical Involvement

Our church is a member of a number of ecumenical bodies, taking an active part in all. We are in the World Methodist Council, an organization of churches with ties to the Wesleyan tradition. We are members of the National Council of Churches of Christ in the United States of America, and our delegates are nominated by the Annual Conferences and elected by the Jurisdictional Conferences. We hold membership in the World Council of Churches, with delegates elected by the General Conference on nomination of the Council of Bishops. And we are members of Religion in American Life, an interdenominational and interfaith agency which directs attention to church attendance and loyalty to one's faith. All these agencies receive financial support from our church on ratios established by their governing boards and constitutions. The United Methodist Church is rightfully proud of its active part in the founding and carrying forward of these ecumenical bodies.

Summary

This, then, is the administrative structure of The United Methodist Church. It is an extremely complex bureaucracy. This is not the passing of a judgment, but the stating of a fact. In the concluding chapter I will deal with the question of the value or lack of value in this organization, and possible alternatives to it.

Chapter VIII

CHURCH PROPERTY

Is it possible for a church to function in the modern world without also being a property owner? The answer to that question is perhaps yes if a new church, from its very inception, were to adopt as one of its basic doctrines a prohibition against the holding of property. In theory such a policy would keep a church from becoming entangled with all the problems which go with owning property, and would free it to carry out its mission in the world. But the fact is that a decision not to own property also puts limits on the carrying out of the mission, and in fact may circumscribe it very severely, especially in the kind of corporate society in which we live today.

John Wesley seemed to take a pragmatic approach to this from the very beginning. One of his societies needed a meeting place; there was one available, and he said, "Let's buy it." But Wesley was also a very wise man who knew it was important to establish legal means which would ensure that the property would be used for the intended purpose, and not be misused or dissipated. The system worked out by Wesley remains the basis of the property-holding system of The United Methodist Church today, as well as other churches which have adopted some of its provisions.

The Trust Clause

In the Roman Catholic Church, the title to the local church property is held by the bishop of the diocese. Most states provide in their laws for a "corporation sole," a legal device by which a Roman Catholic bishop can enjoy all the benefits of being a corporation in regard to his holding title to real estate. Thus, title to any Roman Catholic church is clearly not in the hands of the local congregation.

In nonconnectional or more strictly congregational type churches, such as the Baptist, the title to the church property is held by the local church itself and controlled completely by the congregation.

In The United Methodist Church, we come in between these two. The title to a local church building is actually held by the local church itself, but it is held *in trust* for the whole United Methodist Church, and is subject to the rules of its *Discipline*. The statement is sometimes made that United Methodist churches are "owned by the conference." This is not true. The local church owns its own property, subject to certain checks and balances in the *Discipline*. One of the key ones is the trust clause (Par. 2503).

The trust clause is a simple paragraph which is to be included in every deed of property secured by a local church and which makes it clear that the local church holds the property in trust and in accordance with the *Discipline*. One of the basic reasons for the trust clause is to give assurance to the person who donates money for land or building of a local United Methodist church that this money will always be used for that or a similar church purpose.

Two personal illustrations may help clarify the importance of this. One day when I was a district superintendent, I received a letter from a man who was interested in buying a piece of property in the San Juan Islands. When he had checked the title, he found it was in the name of a local Methodist church. I did not know that such a church existed or had ever existed, although checking in the records showed that over fifty years before, there had been a church at that place. I was able to initiate abandonment procedures (discussed later in this chapter) for the property and sell it to the man. The proceeds of the sale then went, by order of the conference, into district church extension funds to provide land or buildings for some other congregation in the vicinity. Thus, the $5 or $10 gifts made by devoted laypersons to provide a church in that place were not lost, but were conserved for the church purposes for which they were originally given, and will be conserved indefinitely.

The other case was similar, except that one of the last elected local church trustees still survived. The would-be purchaser wanted to buy the property from him, although no local church organization had existed for forty years. The lone trustee was ready to make the deed and receive the price himself. But the representative of the title insurance company knew enough about United Methodist law to know that this man could not convey a good title, and so he checked with my office. Once again, property and its proceeds were conserved for the use of the church. This points to a practice which every superintendent should follow: that of putting a copy of the property provisions of the *Discipline* into the hands of every title insurance company in the district, and being sure they have an understanding of our procedures.

Important as the trust clause is, its absence in a deed does not in any way absolve a local church of its responsibilities to the connectional church. The trust clause is simply a way of formalizing in black and white the actual status of property in the United Methodist Church. Paragraph 2503.5 makes it clear that when a local church acts like a United Methodist church by using its name and customs and accepting ministers appointed by a bishop or employed by a superintendent, its property is held subject to the *Discipline* regardless of the absence of the trust clause in the deed.

One further point should be made concerning the trust clause: it reserves no right or interest to the grantor, but solely to the grantee. That is, a seller of property to the church has no right to try to claim the property back because the church may quit using it for church purposes; the clause is to protect the church, not the seller.

Compliance with Local Law

As a general rule, where local laws concerning property conflict with provision of the *Discipline*, the local laws prevail. For instance, the *Discipline* provides that a deed may be signed by any two of the officers of its trustees; but if a state law requires the signatures of three officers for a valid deed, then the state laws prevails. However, there are limits to the application of this principle, as the *Discipline* makes clear:

Provided, however that this requirement shall not be construed to give the consent of The United Methodist Church to deprivation of its property without due process of law or to the regulation of its affairs by state statue where such regulation violates the constitutional guarantee of freedom of religion and separation of Church and state or violates the right of the Church to maintain connectional structure; and *provided* further, that the services of worship of every local church of The United Methodist Church shall be open to all persons without regard to race, color, or national origin (Par. 2506).

This provision is especially important in view of efforts made in recent years by some states to pass laws with the intention of contravening the property provisions of connectional churches such as ours. What usually happened was that a number of persons in some local churches, being out of sympathy with the social views of the national leadership of the denomination, have sought for state laws which would allow local congregations to pull out of the denomination and take the property with them, provided that a certain percentage of the local membership voted to do so. But the courts of our land have reasserted that such legislative attempts are unconstitutional, being a deprivation of due process and a violation of our views of the separation of church and state. This view was clearly set out back in 1872, in the leading United States Supreme Court case of Watson *vs.* Jones. The theory back of this position is basically this: you don't have to join a church; when you do so, it is presumably with knowledge of how the church functions, how it holds its property, and so forth. If you don't like these provisions, you can try to change them, but failing that, you have to live with them or leave the church; the courts will not intervene in the internal affairs of churches to remedy things that a member thinks unfair.

This basic view has been reiterated again and again by the

courts, and is the well-accepted law of the land. It is this view which the *Discipline* states in its exception to the general principle that local laws prevail.

Property of General Conference, Annual Conferences, and Districts

The 1972 General Conference provided that property held at the General Conference level, which was formerly vested in the Board of Trustees of The United Methodist Church, should henceforth be vested in the General Council on Finance and Administration. So this latter body now carries out this property-holding function in addition to its administrative and fiscal functions.

In each Annual Conference there is a Board of Trustees of twelve persons—⅓ laymen, ⅓ laywomen, and ⅓ clergy. This board administers funds and property received from gifts, donations, and bequests, and takes any necessary legal steps to safeguard Annual Conference property. One of their major responsibilities is the holding of properties which have been declared abandoned by the conference. This latter procedure, described in Paragraph 2548, is an important one in connectional United Methodism and merits a brief description at this point.

The procedure is ordinarily used when a local church property has been abandoned; that is, people have moved away, services have ceased, the organization is no longer current, a minister is no longer appointed. In such a case, the Annual Conference may declare the property abandoned after securing the consent of the bishop, a majority of the superintendents, and the local district Board of Church Location and Building. If local trustees remain, they are then under obligation to dispose of the property according to the instructions of the Annual Conference. If there are no local trustees, or if they for any reason fail to follow instructions, then the Annual Conference trustees are empowered to dispose of the property according to the Annual Conference direction.

But another use of this provision, seldom invoked but nevertheless important, is in connection with a dissident congregation. Suppose an entire local congregation, including all the trustees, become disenchanted with the church at large, withdraw from its membership and proceed to organize their own community church, and yet keep right on using the church building as though it were their own. There are several things the pastor and district superintendent might do in such a case, but one thing the Annual Conference may do is declare the church discontinued or abandoned, thus giving the trustees of the Annual Conference the legal authority to execute a deed to the property. They may end up selling it to the dissident congregation, but they have maintained the connectional property rights of the church.

The Annual Conference trustees also have the authority to purchase an episcopal residence for the bishop in cooperation with other Annual Conferences in the episcopal area. Such action is to be taken only after appropriate authority has been granted by the Annual Conference on the recommendation of the Episcopal Residence Committee.

On the district level, there is optional provision for a district Board of Trustees to hold title to a district parsonage. Sometimes, however, title to such parsonages is held by the conference Board of Trustees, rather than establishing district boards of trustees. Perhaps a more important district body concerned with property is the district Board of Church Location and Building. In large districts, there may be two such boards. Each is made up of the district superintendent and three ministers and three laypersons who are nominated by the superintendent and elected by the Annual Conference. This board has the important responsibility of approving all proposed new church sites and parsonage sites, and the purchasing, building, or remodeling of church structures. If this board disapproves of plans, the local church cannot proceed, although it has a right of appeal to the Annual Conference. In actual practice, the board seeks to provide friendly help to the local church and does not so much lay down the law as provide helpful alternatives to courses of action which it deems unwise.

Local Church Property and Building Procedures

As indicated earlier, title to local church property rests with the local church in trust for the Annual Conference, and the local

Board of Trustees is immediately responsible for it. The Board of Trustees consists of from three to nine persons, at least two-thirds of whom must be members of The United Methodist Church. In view of the disciplinary provision which requires all members of the Administrative Board to be members of the local church, it seems rather strange that up to a third of the trustees need not be members of any church at all. The trustees serve three-year terms, in classes to ensure continuity. They are amenable to the Charge Conference or, if their church is part of a circuit, to the Church Local Conference, consisting of the members of the Charge Conference who are also members of their local church. Thus, the board carries out its responsibilities basically at the direction of the Charge Conference. When so authorized, it may proceed to incorporate the church under the *Discipline,* or deal in property and building, accept or reject gifts, bequests, and devises, and to do all other necessary things relating to the property of the local church. If a trustee withdraws from membership in The United Methodist Church, his or her membership automatically terminates, and if the trustee refuses to sign a legal document as directed by the Charge Conference, he may have his office declared vacant by the conference by majority vote.

While the Board of Trustees has general authority over the use of the church property, it is subject to some restrictions. It cannot, for instance, deprive any official organization of the church of its rights to legitimate use of the property; nor can it prevent or interfere with the pastor in the use of the property for religious services or other proper meetings or purposes recognized by the law, usages, and customs of The United Methodist Church; nor are the trustees to permit the use of the building for religious or other purposes without the consent of the pastor or, in his or her absence, the district superintendent.

If a local church wishes to purchase real estate, it is required to provide ten days' notice of a session of the Charge Conference, at which time a majority vote of the conference must be secured; furthermore, the written consent of the pastor and district superintendent is required prior to the transaction. If it wishes to sell or mortgage real estate, similar notices, meetings, and approvals must be secured.

If the church is contemplating a building project, it may either elect a building committee or commit the project to the trustees. In either event, the procedure for building (Par. 2543) is carefully designed with checks and balances along the way which endeavor to ensure that the building committee is bringing the whole church along with them as they progress in their plans, and to ensure that the plans are well conceived and properly financed.

An interesting question is raised by the disciplinary requirement for the written approval of the pastor and district superintendent on all these property matters. Is the intent of this provision to enable these officials to have a check on matters of form, to ensure that the *Discipline* has been observed correctly in the transaction? Or is it the intent that these officers are to exercise their judgment on the very wisdom of the project, withholding their approval if they don't think it's a good idea? Probably different pastors and superintendents conceive their role differently at this point, but the language of the *Discipline* seems to put no limitation on the full exercise of their own discretion and judgment.

The Board of Trustees is usually considered one of the prestigious positions in the local church, but it is also a position of hard work and great responsibility for those who take it seriously. If the roof leaks or the heat doesn't come on in winter, who wants to come to church?

Church Institutions

Although most of the schools, colleges, hospitals, and homes sponsored by the church are not directly run by it, the *Discipline* nevertheless lays down some minimal guidelines for what we ordinarily call "church institutions." These guidelines provide that trustees of such institutions shall be at least twenty-one years of age, and that three-fifths of them shall be members of The United Methodist Church. However, any Annual Conference may reduce that requirement to a simple majority for a particular institution. This takes a three-fourths vote of the conference. The *Discipline* also requires that the trustees must be nominated,

151

elected, or confirmed by a governing body of the church, or by a body to whom this has been delegated. Other than these basic requirements concerning the trustees, the church does not exercise direct control over most of its institutions, which are separate corporate bodies directing their own affairs.

Summary

All told, the various corporate bodies of our church and their trustees own property (mostly local church) valued in billions of dollars. To manage this vast property in such a way that the mission of the church is enhanced is a fundamental responsibility of every trustee.

Chapter IX

JUDICIAL ADMINISTRATION

In every association of human beings there needs to be a way of resolving disputes and differences of opinion concerning guilt or innocence and varying interpretation of basic law. In ancient times the king made the laws, executed them, and judged the people charged with violating them. But the growth of democratic philosophy in the Western world brought with it the concept of separation of powers, and the United States Constitution is built upon that concept. So it is in The United Methodist Church, with an independent judiciary built into its Constitution, providing an important democratic safeguard for all its members.

The Judicial Council

The one-time classic description of the United States Supreme Court—"nine old men"—hardly applies to our Judicial Council. There are nine members, not all of them old, and at this writing two of the members are women. Furthermore, unlike our Supreme Court, the members are ineligible to begin a new quadrennium after they reach seventy. Judicial Council members are elected for eight-year terms rather than life, and they receive no pay for their work.

Members of the Judicial Council are elected by the General Conference from a slate of nominees submitted by the Council of Bishops. The slate contains three times the number of names to be elected. Nomination may also be made from the floor. The General Conference also elects six lay alternates and six ministerial alternates, to be available to serve in case of vacancies arising in the council, which consists of five ministers and four laypersons. In line with the separation of powers theory, members of the Judicial Council are ineligible to be members of the General or Jurisdictional Conferences, or to serve on any general or jurisdictional board, or to do administrative service in any connectional office. The Judicial Council of the former Methodist Church ruled in a split decision in 1962 that this clause did not prevent membership on the Council by a district superintendent or other administrator within an Annual Conference (Decision 196).

While the Judicial Council bears marked similarity to the United States Supreme Court in its power to interpret the law and its right to declare legislation unconstitutional, it does not receive questions in the same manner as the Supreme Court. The Court basically hears cases that come from the lower courts, and has no jurisdiction over deciding general questions of law. A very small percentage of the Council's work is likely to be concerned with appeals from the lower "courts" of the church. The great bulk of its work is in deciding questions of law and constitutionality which are posed to it by a variety of bodies within the church whom the *Discipline* authorizes to seek such decisions. In this respect, then, the Council is almost more of an administrative tribunal than it s a court as that term is used in civil law.

Not everyone or everybody in United Methodism has the right to have a matter decided by the Judicial Council. The groups who can bring a matter to the Council are fairly limited, as spelled out in Paragraphs 2607-2615. Basically two routes are provided for: an appeal, which is more in the nature of an adversary proceeding and may require as few as a fifth of the members of a body to bring to the Council; or a request for a declaratory decision, in which bodies from the Annual Conference up may request a ruling as to the constitutionality, meaning, application, or effect of the *Discipline* or other acts of the General Conference.

In addition, the Judicial Council automatically reviews all decisions of law made by bishops in the various conferences, "upon questions of law submitted in writing in the regular business of a session" (Par. 2612).

Former decisions of the Judicial Council and of the Judicial Council of The Methodist Church are considered "persuasive as precedents" in the decision of cases before the Council. When the Judicial Council makes its decision, it is final. However, it has a duty to report any findings of unconstitutionality immediately to the General Conference, so that the General Conference can take remedial action. This procedure has great advantages over the procedure in civil government, where the legislative body ordinarily has no way to get a completely authoritative ruling on constitutionality at the time the legislation is being considered.

The decisions of the Judicial Council are published regularly, and may be obtained through The United Methodist Publishing House. Digests of all decisions of the Judicial Council of the former Methodist Church up through May of 1964 appear in the 1964 Methodist *Discipline* (Par. 1702). It is to be hoped that future *Disciplines* will continue to carry such digests, since the Judicial Council decisions represent the law of the church.

The United Methodist Church has reason to be grateful for the Judicial Council as it carries out its extremely important function within the church.

Trial Procedures

The opening phrase of the disciplinary Paragraph 2624.1 on trials says this: "Church trials are to be regarded as an expedient of last resort." This certainly expresses the sentiment of most United Methodists, for there is something highly distasteful and incongruous about the church putting someone on trial, and a church dedicated to the process of reconciliation surely ought to find other ways to resolve its differences. However, there are occasions, thankfully rare, when intolerable impasses are created which can only be resolved by means of a trial. I have been involved in one trial as counsel for the church, and in four others as presiding officer, and though they were distasteful experiences in many ways, some of the participants remarked afterward that it was a healthy thing to have had the trial instead of sweeping things under the rug as we often tend to do in the church. A trial may even be a redemptive experience if it is approached by its participants in that spirit.

There are basically four offenses for which any member of the church, lay or clergy, may be tried (Par. 2621). They are "*(a)* immorality; *(b)* crime; *(c)* disobedience to the Order and Discipline of The United Methodist Church; *(d)* dissemination of doctrines contrary to the established standards of doctrine of the Church." In addition, clergy, bishops, diaconal ministers, and local pastors can be tried on grounds of "practices declared by The United Methodist Church to be incompatible with Christian teachings; . . . failure to perform the work of the ministry; . . . indifference; racial or sexual harassment; . . . relationships and/or behavior which undermines the ministry of another pastor."

The basic procedures of the *Discipline* provide for any alleged charges first to be investigated by a committee of the accused's peers (although in the case of an accused bishop, neither the investigating committee nor the Trial Court is made up of bishops, but of traveling elders; here is one place where the concept of the episcopacy as an office and not an order takes on meaning, for the traveling elders *are* the bishop's peers) who, if they find reasonable grounds for the complaint, are to draw up formal charges. A disciplinary statue of limitations (Par. 2623.1 *b*) rules out bringing charges on offenses which are more than two years old.

The accused is entitled to counsel, who is to be clergy in case of a bishop or elder, or either clergy or layperson in case of laity. The *Discipline* sets out rather elaborate details concerning trial procedures, including such items as the right of counsel for either side to disqualify prospective members of the court by peremptory challenges or challenges for cause. Every effort is made in the disciplinary provisions to provide fairness in the proceedings.

The 1980 General Conference passed new legislation (Par. 453) which applies only to ordained ministers and sets up a rather complex review process (described in an earlier chapter). The 1984 General Conference added similar procedures for bishops (Par. 513).

Legislation was presented to the 1988 General Conference

intended to mandate the joint review process (Par. 453) prior to presenting charges to an Investigating Committee, but Paragraph 2623.3*b* still requires the district superintendent to convene the Committee on Investigation within sixty days of receiving charges. This would seem to still leave the door open to bypassing the Joint Review Committee if this seemed called for. However, the 1988 General Conference also amended Paragraph 2623.1*a* to require that all charges must be signed by the chair of the Board of Ordained Ministry, which seems at least to *imply* that the joint-review process must first take place. However, this sweeping requirement appears to require that *all* charges, including charges against laypersons or diaconal ministers, for whom no joint-review process is provided, must be signed by the chair of the Board of Ordained Ministry. It is almost impossible to believe the General Conference intended this result. Thus ambiguities in the process remain.

It takes a two-thirds vote of the Trial Court (made up of thirteen members) to convict a person of an offense. The most drastic punishment which can then be given is expulsion from the church.

There are provisions for appeals to be made in all cases.

One of the principal justifications for having a procedure in the church for trials is that it is actually more of a protection for the individual than it is a weapon of the church. In fact, the fourth Restrictive Rule in the Constitution specifically forbids the General Conference from doing away with the right of trial and appeal for anyone in the church. Seen in this light, our trial procedures are more of a guarantee of the rights of individuals within the church than they are a possible instrument of persecution by the institution.

Chapter X

CONCLUSION

To anyone who has read all of this book to this point, The United Methodist Church must seem an immensely complicated mechanism. It is. One of the problems with a book like this, which seek to present a picture of the whole organizational structure of the church, is that the church comes out almost inevitably looking like a great machine, since this is the only way the human mind can grasp the whole picture. It is not a machine.

A mechanism, but not a machine—what is the distinction? A mechanism is simply a way of doing something, a device or method for getting a job done. In this sense, the structure of our church is a mechanism. But a machine suggests the cold, hard meshing of gears, the impersonal grinding out of certain results according to a predetermined pattern. Our church structure is not such a machine. It is actually a great skein of human relationships, formalized in black and white into a book called the *Discipline* by representatives of the whole church, in order to carry out the mandate of mission in a highly corporate and technological society.

In order to see what the structure is actually all about we need to leave our point of perspective which gives us a view of the entire structure and move, like a movie camera zooming in on its subject, into a meeting of a section of a division of one of our great boards. What do we find here? We find a group of flesh-and-blood human beings sitting around a table, earnestly discussing ways of ministering to people in the particular area of responsibility which is theirs. It is this kind of picture, multiplied hundreds of times and extending over all the world, that our bureaucracy is all about. A common human attitude is evident here. People tend to hate the A.M.A., but they love their own doctor; they often have serious reservations about the clergy, but they think their own minister is a good person; and they dislike the church bureaucracy, but the particular part of the church with which they are involved is doing a great job!

This is not said in the naïve assumption that our structure is a perfectly functioning instrument of the Kingdom—far from it. It is subject to Parkinson's well-known law regarding proliferation of personnel, and to various other diseases common to all bureaucracies. The real question that needs to be asked is, What are our alternatives?

One alternative is for the church to quit doing all the things that it is doing. It is probably that there are some functions of some boards or agencies which we could just as well do without—but which ones are they? Get the General Conference to agree on which ones they are, and they could be eliminated. But any real cutback in the program of any church can only be viewed as a desertion of the basic mission which is the reason for the church's existence. This is particularly true of The United Methodist Church, which has always been a "doing" church, never content unless it has been doing the gospel. The alternative of giving up our activism is really unthinkable for United Methodists.

Another alternative is to decentralize the work. This may be possible and perhaps feasible for some of the tasks, but it doesn't eliminate bureaucracy—it simply spreads it out to other levels. Furthermore, there are a number of tasks of boards and agencies that are almost necessarily national in scope; most of the pressing Christian social concerns, for instance, are national and international in impact, and a board speaking at the national level is imperative. Sometimes the reason decentralization of a certain function is not feasible is simply economy—the church can only afford to have one office doing a particular task.

There is always the alternative of streamlining the structure, and everyone is for that. But the practical problems of streamlining are very real. If you want more coordination of effort among the boards and agencies, you amy accomplish this by grouping them into three or four superboards, but you have also added another layer of administration. If you streamline by reducing personnel in so-called strictly administrative posts, you are likely to cut back on coordinating efforts in the process, and this may result in an increase in overlapping efforts. This does not mean that efforts to streamline should not be made—they should be, and constantly.

But let no one think that the most effective streamlining is going to remove the problems of bureaucracy from the doorstep of The United Methodist Church. They are here to stay, an inevitable part of what it means to be in mission in the church in today's society. The order of the day for the politician is Big Government; for the laborer it is Big Labor; for the person in business it is Big Business. If the church is to "live and move and have its being" in that kind of an order, it must put behind it the sentimental illusions of being the "little brown church in the vale," and take its place in mission to the society in which we now live. If this means bigness and bureaucracy, so be it. Let us be thankful that we have the instrument at hand that can make even bigness and bureaucracy servants of our mission.

That instrument is the General Conference, described earlier in this book as one of the most powerful ecclesiastical assemblies on the face of the earth. When the Second Vatican Council met, it made sweeping changes which made headlines around the world. One of the reasons for this was that the council hadn't met for a hundred years—no wonder changes needed to be made! Our General Conference meets every four years, a democratically elected body that we can expect to keep abreast of changes and constantly mold the structure of the church to fit the needs of the present. But the General Conference has sometimes been timid, not so much molding the structure as seeming to be the captive of it.

But the times call for bold action, and the General Conference in the 1990s must be prepared to respond to that call. Part of that call may be to give up our life into the larger life of a more inclusive structure, such as that represented by the Consultation on Church Union. Pray God that when United Methodists respond to that call, it will not be on the basis of fear or timidity, but truly in response to the promptings of the Spirit.

It is an axiom of modern architecture that "form follows function." In other words, you don't build buildings according to some abstract plan and then let the people do the things inside them that the building allows them to do; rather you find out what the people want to do in the building, and then you design it to make it possible for them to function in it most effectively. On the other hand, Marshall McLuhan contends that in communication the form of the message definitely affects the content of the message; he goes so far as to say, "The medium *is* the message."

What does all this say about the structure of the church? The architects' dictum would say to us that our first responsibility is to discover anew what the church is and what its function is (the nature and mission of the church), and then devise structures which will undergird and enhance that function. This needs to be a continuing task of the church. But McLuhan also makes a valid point, and should serve as a reminder that *form* is never simply neutral, but speaks a language of its own.

Another way of expressing this idea is in existentialist terms. The existentialist says, "Existence precedes essence," which is like "form follows function." Or, couched in the language of the church, "the church is what it does." But most Christians could not accept that view, and would hold the conviction that the church *is* something, or at least God intended it to *be* something, and what it *is* ought to determine what it *does*. Or in other words, "function follows form."

These two views are paradoxical, to say the least. But perhaps they give us some clue to the constant tension involved in the task of structuring the church, the Body of Christ—a body intensely human and mysteriously divine.

INDEX

District Superintendent—*Cont'd*
role of, in organizing new
churches, 54-56
term of office, 106-7
Doctrine, official statements of,
38-39

Ecumenical Affairs, Commission
on, 138
Ecumenical relations, 24, 57
Education
church and, 19
see also Crusade Scholarship
Committee; Education,
Division of; Education and
Cultivation, Division of;
Higher Education, Divi-
sion of; Higher Education
and Ministry, Board of
Education, General Board of, 140
Education, Division of, 137
Elder, 79, 80, 108
Episcopacy, 28-29, 108-11
constitutional basis of, 36-38
see also Bishops
Episcopacy, Annual Conference
Committee on, 112, 122
Episcopacy, Jurisdictional Com-
mittee on, 37, 108, 111,
112
Episcopal Church, 119
Evangelical Association, 13
Evangelical Church, 13, 39
Evangelical United Brethren
Church, The (E.U.B.), 12,
13, 15, 25, 27, 28, 30, 37,
39, 41, 82, 107

Confession of faith, 16, 22, 23,
28, 39
declaration of union, 21
Discipline, 82, 91
minister's local church membership, 91, 92
transition period in Plan of
Union, 30, 34, 35
Evangelism, Worship and Stewardship, Division of, 137
Evanston, Illinois, 132, 134

Fellowship, redeemed and re-
deeming, 17, 19
Finance, Committee on (local
church), 64, 71
Finance and Administration,
Council on, 131-32, 140,
148
Frederick, County, Maryland, 13

General agencies
administrative agencies, 129-32
classified, 129
definition of, 128
membership, *see agencies*
program agencies, 129, 135-43
support service agencies, 129,
132-35
General Conference, 25-30, 60,
72, 77, 85, 87, 108, 113-
17, 118, 119, 120, 124,
125, 126, 127, 128, 129,
130, 135, 143, 159, 160,
161
amending the Constitution, 38
boundaries of jurisdiction, 35

167